THE *ZEN* OF
MIDLIFE MOTHERING

Essays from MotheringintheMiddle.com

Compiled and Collected by Cyma Shapiro

Zen

"Our own life has to be our message."
Thich Nhat Hanh, Vietnamese Zen Buddhist monk
teacher, author

The Zen of Midlife Mothering
Essays from MotheringInTheMiddle.com
Copyright © 2013 by Cyma Shapiro
Published By Cyma Shapiro

The Zen of Midlife Mothering: Essays from MotheringInTheMiddle.com edited by Laura Curtis
Edited by Cyma Shapiro
ISBN-13: 978-1494831462
ISBN-10: 1494831465

Cover design by PS Coverdesigns

Table of Contents

The Men

The Myths and Experts

The Writer/Creator

Introduction

by Cyma Shapiro

In my late 40s, after the adoption of our daughter, I stumbled on the book, *The Maternal is Political* - an anthology of powerful and poignant essays written by mothers. At the time, I did not consider myself an activist. However, as both an only child and now, as an adult who had pursued the less taken path of midlife motherhood, I was struck by the fact that after many years of feeling isolated, I suddenly belonged to a group — The Community of Moms — whose collective power and passion just might make a difference...

Around that same time, I began searching for answers to my own midlife mother conundrum — my choice to (re) start a family at an age when others were preparing for retirement, sending their children off to college and reinventing themselves. I found few role models to emulate, and my wide sphere of friends were themselves at a loss for how to deal with my new life. Beset with hormonal changes, aging parents, and my own "middle-age" status, I could firmly say that for the first time in my adult life, I was completely and utterly lost.

As a former journalist, writer, and life-long seeker, I decided to take action, to discover what I was missing. Over the course of more than two years, I networked across the country to find women, like myself, who had also chosen motherhood over 40. I found an eclectic group of nearly 60 women, ranging in age from 41 to 65, and from every socio-economic class, race, religion, creed and family model.

I asked each woman a series of questions: *Why did she start or restart a family over age 40? How did she do this? How did her friends and family feel about her decisions? How did she feel about her life choices? Were she to live her life over again, would she do it the same way, again?* The end result was the creation of the first and only art gallery show dedicated to presenting women who choose motherhood over 40. Consisting of the dramatic black and white photographs of 25 family units, plus accompanying narrative text, **NURTURE: Stories of New Midlife Mothers** began its journey across North America in 2011.

I felt passionate about creating a voice, face, and forum for this group. While a good start, this show was limited by space and audience numbers. I felt that the depth, breadth, and diversity of our journeys — our beautiful and disparate voices — also needed to be heard. Hence, the website for all-things regarding midlife mothers was born.

MotheringintheMiddle.com was a thinly veiled reference to my being in mid-life and my Oreo-cookie status regarding my two generations of children (two in each). The fact is that nearly every (new) midlife parent is in the middle of *something* — two generations of children, two differing adult families, aging parents and young children, perimenopause or menopause, status quo and reinvention, and, of course, living somewhere near the halfway mark of our expected life span.

Here, under one roof, I sought to gather and present as many varied and distinguishable voices as I could find — to revel in the rainbow of experiences and emotions, to explore the wonder of this "brave new world" and all which it encompasses. The beauty of the collected words compelled me to do more.

I believe that midlife mothering/new older-motherhood is the newest chapter in the women's movement — the emerging new face of middle age and women. Well over one million strong and rapidly growing, with approximately 100,000 births to moms 40+ each year, these women are pursuing their lives not collectively, like our younger "soccer moms," but singularly and without fanfare — a Zeitgeist of the times — the result of medical breakthroughs, greater socio-economic freedoms, and changes in traditional family structure(s). And since the Center for Disease Control's statistics only include women choosing motherhood by childbirth, the total number of new older mothers is significantly greater when represented by an increasingly common set of alternative methods including fostering, guardianship, surrogacy, adoption, and blending stepfamilies.

With our ever-changing society, there have been additional bonuses for those choosing new parenting over-40 — men finding themselves fathers at an age when retirement was surely in their sights. There are others who have done a role-reversal in their homes, and chosen to become "Mr. Moms" — stay-at-home dads. The 21st century will be a time for redefining the family model as we know it.

In our two-plus years of existence, *Mothering in the Middle* has garnered more than 570 posts, from nearly 100 contributors and two dozen regulars ranging from well-established/well-known and up-and-coming writers to those new to writing who are just finding their voice. Each contributor has something important to say, to share; each story has something which we hope will resonate with our readers. En masse, we intend to offer encouragement to midlife mothers and fathers, and provide inspiration or support for living both fulfilling and truthful lives. I also hope that we help dispel long-standing societal myths; provide role models for younger women; help redefine notions of women and middle age, and give this growing group a voice.

In this collection, you'll find painful essays delineating love and loss — of children, innocence, and life; spiritual, uplifting works defining the human spirit, the perseverance of women to achieve motherhood at all costs, the unwavering testament to loving children, and of the messiness that life often hands us — ripe with mixed messages, unexpected endings and new beginnings. All of which is done in the name of mothering, of fathering, and of love.

Ten (and then, again, eight) years ago, I felt I had no choice but to find, pursue, and finally get my two children. My journeys to Russia became a spiritual epiphany. In the end, I could finally hold the children I fervently believed were meant to be mine, and who were just waiting for me to embrace them.

In my earlier years, I failed to explore and embrace my womanhood and my motherhood. However, the (not so) simple act of passion — to nurture and to love — ignited a firestorm in me and released a flood of emotions I never knew I had.

I know I speak for so many others when I say that we will stop at nothing — absolutely, positively nothing — to become mothers and fathers, when our time is right.

Be Yourself

by Rachel Snyder

The journey of mothering is like no other,
and it's all too easy to get lost in it.

Right now,
set a conscious intention
to carry every bit of who you are
into your role as a mother.

Promise yourself
that you will embrace your shortcomings
and your missteps
and you will never beat yourself up
for doing the very best you can.

Once you settle into being your authentic self,
you cannot help but become
a one-of-a-kind, original,
remarkable mom.

Don't compare yourself
with any other mother you know,
including your own.

Your genuine mothering path
will have a feel
and flavor and tone
that are yours and yours alone ~
and it just may open you up in new
and unexpected ways.

You may be happy and sad — all in the same day.
You may find yourself more creative, more expressive, more loving.
Other times you might feel angry and sometimes, yes,
you may very well be afraid.

Take these opportunities to know yourself
more deeply.
Consider what feels right for you
as well as for your child.

To revel in being a mother,
you must first celebrate
the unique and beautiful individual
that you are
and always have been.

THE WOMEN

"Motherhood has a very humanizing effect. Everything gets reduced to essentials."

Meryl Streep, actress

Dear Mama:
A Letter to My Daughter's Birthmother
by Jane Samuel

Years ago, as I held my new daughter in my arms, feeding her in the dark of our bedroom in the hopes that her fretful, busy body would settle into sleep, my heart welled with emotions and my mind turned to the woman who birthed this child. Tears streaming down my cheeks, I thought about the pain a woman must face in the giving away of her offspring. Years later, I still think about this woman, who brought my daughter into the world but couldn't keep her. And certainly her daughter, now my beloved youngest, has thought of her many, many times. This letter, written solely by me, is a compilation of some of my thoughts and some things my daughter has wondered.

Dear Mama,

Can I call you that? Mama? I know you are not *my* mother, but that is what she would have called you if she had been permitted to. Had she stayed in your arms, in your home, never finding her way to that gate and thus, that Spartan, sweltering-in-summer, freezing-in-winter room of crying, hungry, abandoned babies. Unlike me, she would have said it with the right tonal inclination, parroting back your words as you taught her with thought, word, and deed who you were — her Mama.

Mama, I have so much to say. So many questions and so many answers. Some for me but most for her. Perhaps

19

you have some too? You should.

First can you tell me, tell her, who you are? Entirely, in every cell of your being. Are you a wife, tied to your husband, and his family, in the traditional, filial way? Or are you single, not ever planning to be mother but left that way after some human-need-driven encounter amidst some backward industrial city of the great China?

Are you a mother of others? She says you are. "Nine: five boys and four girls," she still insists, though how she could know such information is beyond me. She is, I suppose, the missing tenth. But I, believing less in quantum physics and cellular memory, and more in cold hard facts, think perhaps you are mother to one by now, a boy born after her. If you were lucky in the "Chinese way." And, perhaps, the distant *birth* mother of other girls — living where?

Are you Han? Miao? Dong? Northern, Southern, migrant worker, or rural farmer? Poor communist or emerging capitalist? Is your hair straight and coarse like a horse's mane or dry and wavy like hers? Did you give her this soft, cool skin, the color of milk-tea, and curling plump Buddhesque earlobes, or are these her birthfather's genes? And did you, before sending her off to her next life, kiss this skin, stroke this hair, and suck — as I am wont to do — those fleshy morsels dangling from the ends of her ears on either side of her precious face?

Next, tell me — her — us, why and how this *all* came to be? Why did you "abandon" her and how did you do it? Was it voluntary, part of some master plan to pass this child by in favor of another, a boy? Or was it a hasty decision carried out only after all other options had been ticked off as impossible? Was it driven by money, by power — his family's, not yours — or simple need?

And, perhaps most importantly to her, do you miss her? Do you think about her? Do you yearn with every part of your soul — as she did for you for years — to see her, hold her, and know her? Or have you set her aside in a dark, ill-used, part of your heart, pushing the memories of her down every time they try to surface above the din of your day because it is just too hard not to?

Now for the answers I promised you. Yes, she is beautiful, inside and out, from her wide duck-like feet to her broad shoulders, from her full mouth to her double-crowned head, from her compassionate soul to her intuitive spirit. And she is a good daughter: helpful, responsible, and most of all so loving , though it took a while to bring down the wall that her heart had built to protect itself from further pain. She is smart too, quick with her wit when in the mood, good with sums, and a real problem solver. She is strong and athletic and musical too. She is, in a word, a *blessing*.

And, yes, she does remember you. How, I do not know, but some say our cells even have memories back to conception. Growing in you for nine months, being with you even for the few weeks she was, she came to know you — your voice, your smell, your body's ways. And she has carried that with her to her new life, yearning for you to come back and be her mother. Why? Perhaps because she could not understand how it came to be that she was born of one woman in Asia and raised by another woman in North America. Perhaps because she had to grieve you before she could put you aside and love me. Perhaps because she believed, for a long while, you were the good mama (who birthed her) and I the bad mama (who "took" her from China), until she was able to accept me as a good mama too who did love her.

Sometimes I have wished we could find you. But I

know that is next to impossible, and as she and I have talked she has come to know this too, as hard a fact as it is. Perhaps it is the impossibility of this that makes it safe to dream of meeting you, having you know her and her know you. Because as much as I want to heal her of whatever bits of loss still tug at her heart, I would not, could not, give her back to you. She is my daughter, and our bond after years of love and work is stronger than blood — I think.

Before I end this and tuck it aside, un-mailed, I want to thank you. I imagine there were choices you could have made that might have been less open-ended and left you with a different pain. I hear that this is common in China, to find out one is carrying a girl and end the pregnancy. Instead you chose life for this child. And because of that choice I am blessed with her as my daughter. Please know I have loved her from before I ever met her and I will love her forever, never forsaking her, or treating her less than fully as a part of my being.

Xie Xie Ni,

Her Mama

Peace During Midlife

by Monique Faison Ross

Nervously, after my adult daughters were already told what was happening, or more accurately, had figured it out on their own, I sat my 19-year-old son down to have "The Talk." "Mom, what?" he said with growing anxiety. "Just *tell* me." And, so I did: "Leah and I are dating." (Leah is a woman, of course). With a long deep sigh of relief, I had finally said it.

I stared at him, waiting for his reaction and my presumed need to defend my reasons. I was well-prepared to explain why, at this juncture in my life, my relationship with Leah had changed my entire world and would, in turn, change theirs. I wanted to explain that it was not just an overused cliché that spills out of the mouths of many couples, but that Leah did, in fact, complete me.

I also knew that I would now be able to give my children what I had struggled to provide for over 25 years: a loving, respectful, accepting, and secure home environment for them to finish growing up in, to visit with their future children and to come home for holidays. A place where each person would be valued, respected, and unconditionally loved by the parents in the house.

I now felt a tranquil serenity that I had observed for years in others' lives, but had eluded me. Leah had given me the gift of relieving much of the emotional burden that can come with parenting children, young or old. Leah helped me see another viewpoint. Leah helped me be my best so that I could be available for them when needed, and step back and let life unfold, when required. I believed with everything that was in me that if there were two parents in a household, no matter what gender, that they be the best parents possible. All of which brought me back to that moment.

"Oh mom, I knew that already," he said casually. "You did?" I asked, more confused than ever. After all, I had rehearsed my speech numerous times. I wanted to ensure that each child would know what Leah and I shared, and what the relationship meant to both of us.

While all of my explanations were not needed, I said them anyway — three more times, for each of my three other children. But, this time, revealing my truth, I was alone with my son.

Here I was, breathing a sigh of relief from the unburdened stress of having to tell him that I had, well, *switched teams*. I thought I was making a huge confession which would change the course of our world forever. He, however, looked at me as if I was behaving like my usual over-reactive-mothering-self. I felt a bit silly after I had worked myself into a frantic state. He shared that he really liked Leah and that all was good (meaning, as teens tend to describe their state of mind as "just fine"). With that last statement, he turned and walked away. And we carried on as we always did with our routine household activities. One by one, the reactions were the same; the result the same, too. One by one each of the kids conveyed how indescribably happy they were — for me, for us, and *for all of us*.

Over and over, I worried, too, about the reactions from others — that my teen would be harassed by his teen-friends; that my fourth child, the youngest, might not be able to withstand the sometimes harsh comments; that our lives might appear as if we, too, expected our children to "jump fences." That my adult daughters living their own lives in different cities would be embarrassed that, yet again, I had gone against societal norms and carved out my own happiness; our family life seemed void of the *typical* family experience. I felt guilty that my children had to continually, for all of their existence, be the unique family. But just the opposite happened. My friends embraced Leah with open arms. My children's friends were excited for our family. A select few enthusiastically attended our wedding. My children's closest circle of friends never missed a beat, and none made any vicious comments. It appeared as if our love wasn't lost on anyone who loved us.

Leah and I had worked together for just under seven years, both of us in relationships which just didn't fit and just didn't last. During our friendship, we would talk for hours. Sometimes accidental attachments remain long-term friendships. But when you sprinkle in a natural chemistry and add the strength of unwavering commitment, you have a romantic courtship that has been forged and is built to last.

This is what I hoped to show my children. I desperately wanted them to know and see how contented I now felt and how every day, I am a better me. I am a better mom, wife, daughter, and person. I am better because there is a serenity and peace of mind that comes with building a life with the right companion.

The realities of marrying in your mid-40s (esp. for the third time) can't belie the life experiences that each person brings to the relationship. Nearly 20 years ago, my first marriage ended in a very public spectacle which produced grave results. My children were left almost parentless with no one to nurture, love, and guide them.

Now, I felt excited that at age 47, with my four children, we would all "get it right." I would have the peace that comes from a purposeful, committed and loving partnership. The children would have the solid foundation I'd always hoped to offer them.

I had finally made a life choice to share my dreams with my true companion. I did not allow the fact that she is a woman dictate whether that was acceptable or not. Now, I could feel safe in the cocoon that Leah and I would build for our newly-formed family and *our* four children.

I would not want to spend the rest of this journey with anyone else but my wife, Leah. Once my four children gave their blessings and were happy, the rest of the world and its opinion no longer mattered.

Second Chance

by Janice Eidus

Twelve years ago, in middle age, you and your husband begin the process of adopting a child from Guatemala. You're assured by your lawyers that the adoption will go quickly, and that within a few months, you'll be a mother. Still, you're intimidated by the seemingly endless mounds of paperwork, and by how you must be fingerprinted and meet numerous times with social workers and lawyers. You assure yourself that it's all worth it to become the mother of a child who needs you, and whom you need.

But there are legal snafus and political problems in Guatemala, and the adoption slows down. Way down. More endless paperwork. More endless meetings. Still, the adoption doesn't move forward. Among other things, there's a clerk in Guatemala who must stamp some of your papers, and that clerk is away on a long vacation, due back when, no one seems to know.

Throughout all this, there's something else bothering you. You're feeling ill. You've always had medical issues, among them, chronic, debilitating coughs that last for months at a time; rashes on your arms and legs that also come and go; needing to use the bathroom too many times a day, more than seems "normal."

Now your cough is so bad, you frequently have to remove yourself from buses and trains and social occasions because of it. You need to use the bathroom so often it's difficult to go out to see friends or do errands. You fear that you're becoming housebound and will have to stop the adoption process that you've labored so hard and so long on because you'll be too ill to care for a child.

You've been seeing doctors your entire life. Your mother brought you to doctors when you were a child. "She'll grow out of these things," she was assured. As an adult, you continue to seek help. One doctor tells you, "These things make you *you.*" Another says, "You're depressed. See a shrink."

But now the stakes are too high for you to accept that your symptoms won't go away. You want to become a mother too fiercely. You'll do whatever it takes. You return for the umpteenth time to your internist and tell her how sick you feel. "Okay," she sighs, "I'll send you to another G.I. specialist." She's as weary of you as you are of her.

You meet with the new doctor and recount your woes. She asks if you've broken any bones, if you've had gum problems, if your night vision is poor. Affirmative to all.

"I know what you have even before we do tests," she says. "You have celiac."

You've heard of celiac, but she needs to explain to you that it's an autoimmune illness that one has from birth. It damages the lining of the small intestine and prevents it from absorbing parts of food that are important for staying healthy. The damage is due to a reaction to eating gluten, which is found in wheat, barley, and rye.

You must be on a completely gluten-free diet for the rest of your life. You discover that gluten is everywhere - hidden in foods by a myriad of names, and even in your lipstick. If your gluten-free food is contaminated by food or silverware that has touched gluten, you'll feel sick. You and your husband now keep an entirely gluten-free home.

You tell your friends about your illness. One of them, less supportive than the others, says, "It sounds like a death sentence."

Meanwhile, the adoption process has slowed even further — if that's imaginable — due to changing adoption laws in Guatemala. You write letters to U.S. politicians asking them to get involved, but none do. There are rumblings that adoptions from Guatemala will be completely closed before yours even has the chance to go through.

"We just need the chance to become parents," you say often to your husband. "Just the chance." You are by now in great despair of ever becoming a mother.

Then, finally, when you've almost reconciled yourself to it never happening, the new adoption laws in Guatemala are overturned, and you're shown the photograph of the beautiful ten-day-old girl who is to become your daughter. "I love you, I love you," you whisper to the photograph. But it's still a long year from then - before all the paperwork is approved and you're allowed to bring your daughter home with you.

After a few months of her being home, you see a nutritionist who specializes in celiac. You tell her, "I worry that my daughter will be frightened by my illness as she grows older. And that her life will be too circumscribed living in a gluten-free home. I worry that she'll grow to hate the food I serve her. I worry that she'll grow to hate me."

The nutritionist says, "Relax. Your fears aren't only about the food, are they? Don't worry. She'll grow up loving your food because it's the food she knows. And when she wants a yummy gluten-filled cupcake in the outside world, she can have one. And, oh, of course," she smiles warmly, "she'll love you, celiac and all."

And then you see how lucky you are — to have been given two second chances at living the healthy and loving life you've long wished for — by at last becoming a mother, by at last becoming well.

Older Mom, Growing Older
by Barbara Herel

The average life expectancy for women in the U.S. is anywhere from 73.5 to 86 years of age. As the 49-year-old mother of a four-year-old, if I kick when I am 73.5, I'm going to be pissed.

That said, I always knew I'd be an older mom. When my college friends were getting pregnant in their twenties and thirties, I never felt I was missing out. It was only after marrying Tony that I can truly say I caught "baby fever," and by then I was 40.

"Perfect," I thought. I knew plenty of 40-something women who successfully got pregnant with their 40-something eggs and gave birth to perfectly healthy babies. I would, too. Why not? I didn't look my age. If someone asked, "How old are you?" I'd say without flinching, "I'm 40," and was always secretly thrilled by their reaction: "I thought you were 30!" Oh stop now… If my outsides look 10 years younger than my biological age, I reasoned, shouldn't my insides look just as good?

Apparently, this is not how it works. Needless to say, I now know plenty of 40-somethings with tired old eggs, me and my eggs included.

I was 44 when I looked to domestic adoption as my means to motherhood. The month before our daughter's biological mother gave birth and relinquished her parental rights, I celebrated another birthday. And at 45, I had a beautiful, healthy baby girl to love and look after.

It's only within the last year that I've begun feeling anxious about my age. Maybe it's because the newborn/toddler stage, wrought with sleep deprivation and newfound new-mom worries, was such a blur. I constantly felt my brain stutter through every thought, I'd wind up saying things like, "She sick. Me crying." I'm still amazed I had that much clarity.

But now that Beth is four, it seems I can clearly, if somewhat obsessively, contemplate my demise. Yes, it's all well and fine to look younger than my calendar years, but when I think about my age, the actual number — 49 — and the mortality stats, it's shocking to consider the possibility that I could have only 20 or 30-something years left on this earth.

Shocking and quite unacceptable actually, since this means I might not be around to see my 20- or 30-something-year-old daughter's career take off. Or help her plan her wedding, or see her through childbirth or the adoption process, or be a lunch date away from hearing about all the joys and sorrows that life will undoubtedly send her way.

But here's what's truly upsetting about being average when it comes to dying — I wouldn't be around to see the day my daughter sees her mother, and her biological mother, through a grown-up lens.

What will it be like for her to fully grasp that we were human, just like her? That we were each figuring out our lives, each enduring our own disappointments, missteps, and blunders along the way? I hope she'll look at us with understanding, kindness, and an empathetic eye roll, knowing in her heart that in spite of our inadequacies, and how crazy we drove her, we loved her. So very much and did our best by her. Who knows, maybe she'll discover that we were even right about a few things? Imagine that.

Well, I, for one, don't want to miss it. So, other than trusting that genetics are on my side, and watching out for the errant bus as I cross the street, I have decided that "average" isn't going to cut it.

I recently met with a nutritionist and have started eating a low-glycemic diet. I am now "jawking" or jog/walking, for 30 minutes, three times a week. Sure, it's always nice to have a clear separation of thigh and butt, but these days my focus is on doing everything that's in my control to have a healthy strong body and an energetic life — no matter how long it might be. (Sigh...)

However, I'm shooting for 100. Who's with me?

Self-Invention —
The Bond Among Women of All
Generations
by Suzanne Braun Levine

One thing about being an older mother is that you are constantly reminded of the truism that age doesn't really describe the shape of a person's life. Nor does our place on the family tree, the generation we are assigned to at birth.

When my daughter was born I was 44 — old enough to be her grandmother. When she went to school, I was old enough to be her teachers' (and her friends' parents') mother. At the same time my contemporaries had long since forgotten about coping with babies and young children — they were on to the joys of grandchildren. My most meaningful cohort was other women with children my children's age, but not my age themselves.

In other words, for most of my adult life I have belonged to no generation — or all generations. If anything defined me, it was in the trajectory of my life, not where I was in the timeline of my life. Therefore, even though the teachers were half my age, their insights about my child and their expertise about teaching made for a very intimate and respectful relationship. They had acquired an understanding of children in their short lives that I was in need of at that parenting starting point in my long life.

Only now that I am way beyond bonding with other parents of young children and am just one more "older woman" have I become aware of the ageism that abounds in our culture and the way our accumulated years divide us. More than once, I have been chatting with a young man and catch his eyes floating away over my shoulder. I am rarely asked what I "do," although I am still doing it. And "dear" has become a put-down in my dictionary.

Having experienced the intergenerational community of those years when the age of my child was more meaningful than my own, I don't want to lose that in my Second Adulthood — the new stage of life that we — older mothers, empty nesters, childless-by-choice friends, women in the process of starting over — are all defining as we live it. We are demonstrating that self-invention is a lifelong process. That is a starting point for a bond among women of all generations.

But there are obstacles to finding common ground. One is that we are not in the same place at the same time often enough. That's fairly easy to remedy. The technological barrier is a little harder to work around. Women my age talk of a culture gaps in the workplace; for example, we older workers are used to stepping into a colleague's office to touch base.

To a younger woman, the face at the door is an intrusion; e-mail is the way to go. Technology also enables young women to meet and share and protest in ways that we have a hard time keeping up with. If we are going to "sit down over a cup of coffee" — virtual or not — we will have to meet (or tweet) them halfway.

I believe that women young enough to be our daughters (but aren't) want to connect with us as much as we want to connect with them. I experience it personally in the tense alliance between waves of feminism. We Women's Movement-types complain that the younger ones have abandoned the cause; the younger ones resent what they perceive as our assumption — that we defined the cause for all time. The mass marches that we associate with activism have been replaced by on-line mobilization and actions that we have been slow to sign on to.

Yet when we do engage each other over the issues, they want to know what it was like for us; they want to test their ideas out and get knowing — but not condescending — feedback. And they want to know how it is for us now.

At first I was surprised when a young woman would come up to me after a bookstore reading with two copies of my first book, *Inventing the Rest of Our Lives* — "one for my mother and one for me," they would say — but I came to understand that they wanted to read about their own futures. They understand that we are opening up possibilities that they can look forward to taking advantage of when they get there. Together we can be nourished by a community of women, which has no age requirements for entry.

The Things We Do For Love

by Joely Johnson Mork

I spent a big chunk of my 30s and the beginning of my 40s living in upstate New York. It was an old boyfriend who first summoned me to the Saratoga area from Philadelphia. We thought we could rekindle our once-soulmated high school romance by my joining his grownup life, but that spark sputtered out not long after I arrived. Instead, I wound up single again at age 36, with a new personal vow that I would never again move my life to follow a man.

After that reality check of a breakup, I found my way to the nearby city of Troy, where I finally discovered real work and connected with a sincere group of friends. It was also where I met my husband and (eventually) gave birth to my son.

Unlike most women I know, I never expected to marry or have a family. Growing up in a broken home and something about practicing the "engaged detachment" of yoga since the age of 18 had led me to feel pretty distant from those very human goals. But I did get married, and the man who ultimately changed my mind about that is younger than I am by more than just a few years. On a crisp September wedding day, I am proud to say I was still holding it together at 39, and he was a very fresh-faced 26. The great majority of the time, this age difference has no effect on our marriage or on our lives. But then, not long after our fourth anniversary, a recruiter made a phone call, and the wheels of change started turning.

With a mere five weeks notice, my husband was offered a job that promised to do great things for his still-blossoming career as a software engineer. The only catch was that the exciting new position required our relocation to Seattle, an area where he grew up and where his extended family still lives.

Now, I'm no stranger to big moves. When I was around my husband's age, I moved myself cross-country and up and down the Northeast for work opportunities more than once. Every time it was an adventure, a monetary raise, and another rung up on the editorial ladder. That was my era of monk-like living. I didn't own anything I couldn't quickly jettison, and worked exclusively on a laptop computer that fit neatly into a messenger bag. I was intentionally single and blissfully childfree. My apartment-to-apartment maneuvers were quick and easy, and I moved on with mostly dry eyes.

By the time I hit 40, however, and had established myself as a successful freelancer, I thought for sure that I was done uprooting my life as a method of career development. But the fact was that I had married a man still in that early-career-phase where moving for work makes sense.

Living back in Troy, I had allowed myself to settle deeply into a community (making the connections I had avoided in the past), developing a yoga following, and even buying what had previously eluded me — an actual home of my own. All of this would have to be jettisoned if my husband was to accept the new position.

The real life lesson was, in part, in the challenge of marrying a younger man. With the job offer, it was clearly time for my husband to step forward in his work; it was certainly also an opportunity for my son to be surrounded by loving family he would otherwise see only rarely. To take advantage of these options meant it was again time for me to open myself up to unknown possibilities and follow a man into an unknown future. I wound up making the move as mindfully as I could, despite my reluctance and the tears that fell in abundance this time around.

In 2007, our wedding officiant spoke these words: "Marriage is a spiritual grinding stone. In choosing this particular person to make your life with, you are choosing to be affected. Each of you will be the means by which the other one grows."

The concept of a "spiritual grinding stone" might sound a bit harsh, but it's inarguably apt. All of our interactions — with friends, children, family, and especially spouses — have an impact; they "leave a mark," so to speak. These encounters force us to step (or stumble) outside of our comfort zones. I had to make this move and see this life change as a chance to grow for the two people I love most in the world. At the time, I could not think of a better way to do that than by being the means by which my husband and my family could flourish, even though that process called for leaving a comfortable and familiar life behind and staying open to what the next one would look like.

Are you a Polar Bear Mom?

by Wendy Sue Noah

Are you a polar bear *type* of mom — do you *really* know what that means as a mothering analogy?

Well, I didn't, at least fully.

A few years back, a close friend, Sharon, compared me to a polar bear mom whose main focus was to protect her cubs. It sounded complimentary, and it was something I held in my heart for strength, but not something I fully grasped.

Just a little background for you to help put things into perspective before I share my Oprah "Aha!" moment with you.

Before marriage, I did not have motherhood on my "to do" list. Sounds strange to say now, as a single mom of a tribe of five children, but it is true.

Then I married my now ex-husband, and we produced five children within 10 years. On our spiritual path, we believed that if God was to bless us with a child, that we were going to welcome it — hence no birth control.

With each child, I felt more and more blessed. In the past, I had believed that my career, traveling, partying, etc. was what it was all about. Now I knew true joy — the joy of motherhood.

Fast forward. Right around our 10th anniversary, I began questioning his incontestable control and abuse. He threw me out on the street and took our children to live at his sister's house. Instead of digging a hole to bury myself in, or returning to my hometown of Boston, I found shelter at a friend's home and was given free legal help. Against all odds, I won full custody of my children!

It was at this time, when we were all homeless together in the harsh reality of Los Angeles, that my friend, Sharon, associated me with a polar bear protecting her cubs.

I asked her with all earnestness, "Do you really think I can manage all of this?"

Sharon's reply, "Of course you can, Wendy. You are like a polar bear, and you will do whatever you need to do to protect your cubs."

Fast forward again.

It is a Sunday, years later. My children and I are looking at one another with the restless thought, "What to do?"

So I gather my tribe for an IMAX movie at the Science Center, and we see "To the Arctic." It was here that I finally put two and two together! The movie focused on the Arctic and what life is like for polar bears. Polar bears are such a remarkable majestic species. To see them dance and hug under the iceberg cold waters was truly incredible!

The movie focused on a mother polar bear who had two nursing cubs, but could not find any food. The commentator described how unusual this is, since the mother bears need to nourish themselves in order to nurse more than one cub. In this case, her love filled up her milk for them.

Against the odds, and as they continued on their journey, she fed her cubs and thwarted off the advances of other adult bears.

And then it happened.

In an instant, and at a pivotal point in the movie, this bear became both the star and the conqueror. In the face of an advancing male polar bear, she turned around, faced it and roared with all her might.

RRRROOOOOAAAARRRRR!!!

The male bear literally stopped dead in his tracks, and eventually swam away. Her response was clear: "If you want to eat my cubs, you need to go through me."

It was then that I finally got it — yes! There was nothing in Heaven or Earth that would keep me from protecting my babies. I am, indeed, a Polar Bear Mom, and proud of it!

As I researched the magnificence of the polar bear further, I found that they are of great cultural importance to the Inuit ("Eskimo") people of northern Alaska, Canada, and Greenland. Polar bears are greatly respected for their strength, courage, and spiritual power.

What really touched me, however, is that in Inuit mythology, polar bears frequently shape-shift into human form and back, putting on a white bear coat to take on their grand form. When I look back at the crisis that led me to take on this unstoppable, powerful polar bear manifestation, I see now that I actually shape-shifted in my mind and heart. On the outside, I looked like this petite white woman, but on the inside, the polar bear that I became was doing that RRROOOAAARRR of strength, courage, and spiritual power!

The remarkable point here is that we are all capable of doing this internal shape-shifting! We just need to set our focus clearly, and feel inspired to do so. Whether it is an animal or a human being that inspires you, try to use your imagination and watch the internal shape-shifting happen to you, too!

Menopause

by Maggie Lamond Simone

My son was upset the other night because he realized he'd only practiced piano a couple times throughout the week and his lesson was the next day. He was very hard on himself, and I said, "I'm sorry, honey. You're only nine; Mommy needs to remind you more often. That's part of my job."

"But you're in menopause!" he cried. "You can't remember anything!"

And it hit me. I'm not too young for menopause; my *children* are too young for it. Or, rather, for me to be in it. I just finished telling them how a woman's body makes babies, and now I have to tell them how it stops. It's like the short-attention-span-theater version of life talks. Gee, maybe they'll at least be in middle school before I tell them why my bladder's hanging down to my knees.

At least I'm not alone. I've met many, many moms my age — with young children — going through the same thing. Heck, if they can make a Broadway musical about it, then there's something going on. And what's going on, quite simply, is that we're having kids later. At my son's ball games, I could just as easily be sitting next to a pregnant mom as a fellow hot-flasher.

As one friend says, though, 50 is the new 30, and I'm good with that. Heck, I'd be good if it were the new 49. I feel young, and whatever my body has to go through, it will go through. It's biology, that's all. It's just taking some getting used to. When my mom went through all this, I'd already finished college and commiserated with her over some cheese and a nice Chardonnay — not Lucky Charms and a juice box.

Besides, I've been denying my aging for as long as I can remember (ha! That's a joke, because of course I CAN'T REMEMBER!) When the state fair guy guessed my age three years too high I blamed my husband ("You've got gray hair! Of course he's going to think I'm older! I told you to wait over there!")

When the emergency room doctor had trouble quieting my two-year-old daughter and gave her to me, saying, "Tell Grandma where it hurts," I blamed the truly poor lighting (and lest you misread me, there is nothing wrong with being a grandma. Some of the nicest people I know are grandmas. And I look forward to being one myself… later.).

And when the kids ask why I can't jump on the trampoline with them without peeing my pants, I, of course, blame them.

But eventually there was no more denial. We were all walking through Target one day when I started sweating uncontrollably. My hair became soaked, my neck was dripping, I was shaking, and my knees were weak. My husband watched the whole thing in horror, wondering if I was having a heart attack or merely trying to embarrass him. "What the heck's wrong with you?" he asked as I sat on a display to recover.

I glared at him. "It's a hot flash," I hissed. "You know, those things that I'm 'not really having'?"

And then there are the one-sided conversations we have after the lights go out.

"Honey, it's too hot in here. Open a window, would

you?"

"Okay, now I'm kind of chilly. Can you close it back up a little? Thanks, babe."

"Um, sweetie, I'm sweatin' over here. What about that window?"

"Okay, am I the only one in here with goosebumps? Close the window, already!"

"IT'S SO HOT MY SHIRT IS SOAKED. PLEASE, HONEY. FOR THE LOVE OF GOD, JUST OPEN THE WINDOW!"

So I have to explain all this to the kids, or else they'll think Mommy is sick. Between the hot flashes, night sweats, irritability, weight gain, mood swings, facial hair, hormonal acne, and memory problems... actually, except for the first two, that all sounds alarmingly normal. No wonder they're confused.

Wait — we have a piano?

Ripe
by Valerie Gillies

Autumn is the eternal corrective. It is ripeness and color and a time of maturity; but it is also breadth, and depth, and distance. What man can stand with autumn on a hilltop and fail to see the span of his world and the meaning of the rolling hills that reach the far horizon? —
Hal Borland

Here I am, sitting at the computer trying to write something coherent, while inches away my thirteen year old is melting down at the prospect of the first day of school tomorrow. The ostensible issues: backpack size and choice of clothing for the morning. (Truth: nervous beyond belief.) Another, down the hall, is supposed to be packing for a year abroad, but has abandoned a room that could land me with a health code violation, in order to help her friend pack up for school. In the room recently vacated by my eldest daughter are the beginnings of a wedding gown that I should be working on every waking hour.

I am breathing. Deeply. Slowly. Trying to plant myself in a solid place as the door slams and the tornado comes and goes from my room. I refuse to be swept away. I will not look in the disaster room tonight and wonder, yet again, how on earth it can possibly be cleaned out by next weekend. Or worse, wander into imagining that 20 years from now it will still be like it is, only dustier and covered with spider webs. I will not respond to the repeating questions of why certain things that do not conform to dress code cannot be worn tomorrow. I will stay away from the sewing zone. I will keep my fingers on the keys. And breathe.

Outdoors, it is a stunning evening. There are actual, real life pumpkins in my otherwise barren vegetable garden. While I rued the loss of my tomatoes and chard to deer, the vines crept around, secretly fruiting under enormous leaves. Those big, beautiful pumpkins are now turning orange.

An hour ago, when I went out to the coop, my chickens were arranged on their perches, cooing away contentedly after a day outdoors. The night sounds begin, and I pause to wonder which creatures are waking up in the dusk. In the same zone as the tornado and the room-o-junk, lies unspeakable beauty, things that are truly wondrous. I focus on the late summer evening, warm but not hot, alive but not loud. Lush.

My life is ripe. I have gone enough distance to know that the unpleasant noise and distraction of this evening is merely that. And if I can wait it out for a very short while, the chaos will give birth to opportunity.

Autumn is the season when I reset my life. To my children, as with my earlier self, transitions are accompanied by more fear and anxiety than hope and anticipation. Without my noticing exactly when, the scales have tipped in the opposite direction. I now find times of change to be the easiest in which to do things differently — sort out, discard, clean up, and begin.

When I can breathe and remove myself from the cloud of commotion, I am able to stand on the hilltop, take in the awesome view, and see which tempting paths I would like to try next. And to know that if they disappoint, I don't need to stay on them.

I no longer have the illusion of having forever ahead of me. In its place, I know with certainty that few of the limits I have ever put upon myself were real. I am free to try. And to fail — to be in those less 'successful' moments and find the pleasure in knowing I will go on, life will continue, and it will somehow, in some crooked way, all be okay.

Once the tornado goes to bed, I will have a delicious time where I sit down with the calendar and begin to plot out the next few months. I will choose the things I want to push myself to try. I will decide what I can live without. Mine to savor and enjoy the fantasy, knowing full well that nothing ever turns out exactly the way I intend — which is good.

This year, I am determined to conquer organic chemistry. It whipped me in college, and it's time I got even. It can't be as hard as giving birth, sitting up all night in a hospital room with a sick child, or at the bedside of a dying parent. Last year I learned to exercise. Every day. And enjoy it. So, I confess to feeling somewhat invincible.

I know that somehow, the teenager will be dressed and make it to school in the morning — even if grumbling the whole way. Her older sister will somehow manage to pull herself out of denial to clean and pack her room. The wedding gown will somehow, amazingly, be made. None will be hastened by my anxiety or unhappiness. I will yield to this sensuous evening, and let the feel of it set the tone for another chance at a fresh start.

Mom-on-Demand

by Lori Pelikan Strobel

I am standing at my new desk — a desk that can be raised to a standing height or lowered to a sitting height. I love it! The room that this desk stands in is my office. It has been in a bit of transformation lately — just like my life. The walls are painted the softest of green. A small but dazzling crystal chandelier light hangs from the center of the room. It is pleasant here alone with my own thoughts.

Suddenly I hear the garage door open and footsteps. "Mom, I'm home!" yells my daughter from the kitchen as she loudly drops her book bag, coat, and whatnot that I envision lying in a trail on the floor. My peacefulness is broken by her voice and I am suddenly transported back ten years ago when she would come home from school with the same declaration. Although times have changed, things have a way of staying the same. I am still here whether or not she is.

Finally, I hear, "Mom?" as she nears my office. And, upon finding me, it is like presto! I am "on," just like the cable TV that always slightly glows as it waits to be powered on. She has turned on the Mom-on-Demand remote. Press the button and I am available 24-hours-a-day. My children choose when, how, and where to connect with me. I am always here glowing, softly waiting whether or not I am needed. Nobody brings my children what they want more than Mom-On-Demand!

I hear the dog ring his bell which signals that he wants to go outside. My daughter says, "Hold on, Louie!" I hear her loudly give him hugs and a dialogue of I missed you begins. I love to hear her home from college. Just listening to the sounds she makes gives me an idea as to what she is up to. Now, I hear the shower start and the sounds of her sneakers drop to the floor. They will remain there until she needs them again or until her older sister starts complaining about them being there.

This is just how she leaves her cereal bowl in the sink. I refuse to put it in the dishwasher. It is a battle of the wills. This bowl and the next bowl and next will remain there until there is yelling. Then she sweetly says, "Oh. I forgot." I reach for my glass of water; I can still taste the perfect lovely gluten-free almond horn cookie I had a few minutes ago. That perfect cookie was being eaten peacefully before I became Mom-on-Demand, again.

Now, as my daughter is singing in the shower, I sit here thinking of my life as an empty- nester. I am supposed to travel, supposed to not make dinner if I don't feel like, and supposed to have a full night of worriless peaceful sleep. That has not happened yet.

My 23-year-old college graduate has a wonderful job as a nurse. She has decided to live at home to save money. I am thankful that she is here because on her days off we sometimes hang out together. I still, however, make sure there is food in the house for her, remind her to make her dentist appointment and teach her how to pay her bills. I still listen for her when she drives home from work at 2 a.m. I still worry when I see her sick and she still wants Mom to make her toast with cinnamon and sugar to make her feel better.

The 20 year old, who is now blow-drying her hair, still wants her favorite foods. She still calls me with her stressful days of tests and papers, and she still asks if she should go to the infirmary when sick. She still wants me to make her toast with cinnamon and sugar on it just as she did when she was six years old. My daughters have not really changed much from when they were 6, 10, 16, or over 20. There is always a new motherhood in the offing no matter how old my children or I get.

When they both were at college, my husband and I looked at each other every night and asked "What do we do?" After all the years of driving and worrying, it was finally time to relax and enjoy being without children in the house. And so, we got a puppy! Louie became our newest family member. We started being parents to a young one all over again… potty training, taking him to school, and scheduling play dates with other dogs. Now, we have to be home for the dog! We choose to spend our spare time walking with Louie, sitting in our backyard watching him play, or staying home and watching a movie. I am now Mom-on-Demand for Louie, too!

My daughter peeks her head into my office. "See you later. I'm meeting my friends," she says as she kisses my cheek. I breathe in the scent of her wonderfully washed hair and her signature perfume.

I am still Mom, now and forever, as I sit here in my office trying to figure out where my life is headed. I know one thing for sure: I will always be Mom-on-Demand; I would not have it any other way. I reach for another cookie, gaze out my office window, and contemplate.

Remote off. Mom Out. Power down — until next time.

When Shift Happens At Midlife
by Lisa Garon Froman

NEVER IN LIFE is there a need to call on the power of grace and humility more than at midlife. As we take measure of our lives, we can find ourselves dismayed, discouraged, and disillusioned to find our lives simply no longer fit us. All that we thought we were, no longer makes sense. Suddenly, we don't fit in our own skin, never mind our own clothes. We look in the mirror and see faces, even bodies, we no longer recognize.

At midlife, many of us begin to feel a shift, or an unearthing, as I like to call it. Our jobs may or may no longer interest us in the same way, our relationships with our spouses or partners may have shifted — for better or worse — or even ended.

Maybe the way we mother has changed.

And finally, for some of us, the things that we wore as badges of success no longer keep us warm, no longer offer us a sense of security.

Let's face it. Midlife is a time of turbulence for many of us. Sometimes the turbulence comes from an inner state, sometimes from outside influences. Midlife is a time of undoing and unearthing, a shedding of ourselves as we learn to question. The questions may start small, but invariably grow, like a sprout, seeking, searching, and questioning, all skills cultivated over time. Some of us are forced to do the hard and dirty work quickly, but in the end, the process of shifting, unearthing, will take as long as it takes. It is different for each of us.

This is what my unearthing looked like: Empty nest.

Divorce. Job loss. Move. Like a series of dominoes, one after another, after another, parts of my world collapsed into an ugly, unrecognizable heap of turmoil.

Everything that offered me a sense of security, a sense of myself, evaporated in one seemingly collective poof. My friends and family were horrified and silently awaited my meltdown. And waited. And waited.

For as the structures that shaped my life began to break apart I grew strangely quiet, strangely resilient. And somehow, in the breaking apart, the unearthing, I grew stronger. Centered. Clear.

My unearthing, my dark night of the soul, sent me on a journey to high and low ground, and finally, back to my higher self.

As they say, the journey of a thousand miles starts with a single step. This famous line comes from the ancient Chinese classic, the *Tao Te Ching.* I discovered this masterpiece while on my journey and used its wisdom for regular inspiration.

Now you might ask yourself… what wisdom can a modern middle-aged woman gain from an ancient text? My answer: *a book's worth.*

After all, the *Tao Te Ching* outlines a simple philosophy of life that is focused on compassion, humility, harmony, and moderation. It is a beautiful book full of paradox, like yin and yang, night and day, good and evil. Much like our human existence, it points to the duality of life. Yet it continues to offer hope, inspiration and guidance for creating a more peaceful, meaningful life. Especially at midlife.

So I used the wisdom of the *Tao Te Ching* to reflect on the changes many of us women experience at midlife. And I wrote about it in my book, *Tao Flashes, A Woman's*

Way to Navigating the Midlife Journey with Integrity, Harmony and Grace.

I write about what I believe many midlife women are concerned about. I write about authenticity, living with integrity, harmony.

There is a reason we begin to feel a shift at midlife. I believe it is a calling to our higher selves, to our authentic spirits.

As we enter midlife, we feel a call to return to our true nature, to the person we stuffed away like a shiny prize at the bottom of a Cracker Jack box. She might be hard to find behind the coulds and the shoulds and the well-meaning directives that may have diluted her spirit. But she's there.

When you are lucky enough to find this beautiful child, this magical creature, you must treat her with wonder, welcome her back with giddiness and joy , knowing she is your inner child, your conscience, your voice — and your very best friend and protector.

Welcome her back for she brings clarity. She is your risk taker, the one who has appeared to bring you back to yourself.

Hold on to her and let her lead you home.

Affirm her. And every time you make a choice for yourself… a choice against the status quo… a choice that rings so loudly with authenticity all doubt is silenced, you will feel her presence.

For this risk taker, this beautiful child, this magical creature, is your authentic spirit. And your higher self. Get to know her.

Dating as a New and Single Midlife Mother (Or, How to Ride a Harley Sideways)
by Kristi Rodstrom

Okay, I will oblige you... if these are my golden years, then mine are more the color of "rust-y."

I am a midlife mother. My children are nine and five years old. I am also a single mom, a professional, a daughter, an advocate for my children and, now, add to that list... someone who dates. No, really!

After two and half years of what I'll call "dating atrophy," I found my reentry, my kick-start, my mojo — call it whatever you want, on the back of a Harley. The wind in my face, holding tightly to the waist of a burly man and my responsibilities tucked into (his) safe arms, this singular event was the tonic my soul needed to surge forward. Where I was, and actually continue to be, has literally been one of the most difficult things to navigate; these are complex waters! Dating in one's midlife should include a GPS... Oh, and my reading glasses, since I seem to need those for everything these days.

So, as I check the mirror in my family room for the third time and wait for the doorbell to ring, I contemplate which "hat" I will be wearing tonight. God-forbid I happen to put on the "mom cap" and wipe my date's chin, or my professional fedora and correct his grammar/syntax, or my beret and start my rant. I prefer to call it a "gentle educating," discussing the direction of research about

Autism — a favorite topic of mine. Sadly, I have done all of the above before appetizers were even served.

Upon reflection, the best hat for me is my thinking cap. Same wisdom used in all situations of dating — be considerate, find out about my companion, allow my date to talk... and they all get there. Then, just before I hit him with my heavy artillery, I ask him to put on a hat of his own. Actually, it is more like a helmet!

It is precisely at that moment that I utilize the sports theory that "the best defense is an honest offense." I lay my life's complexities on the line and let him know that I am the poster child for the "red-flag-girl." Picture my date as Andretti's own on his final lap, and me off to the side waving, oh, let's be conservative and say, one hundred red flags. I may be energetic, and my legs in short black short shorts are still hot, but keep in mind... I have two YOUNG children, and it will be thirteen years before my youngest completes high school (God willing...).

Just as a review: to make sure my date on his final lap has clarity, I am a single mom who works a lot; has, at best, two nights a week to go out; and, most importantly, has two young children, one being a sassy little thing headed to either law school or jail (since this is an unknown at this point), and a low functioning Autistic son.

Being as helpful as humanly possible, I feel compelled to let out a blood curdling scream and at the top of my lungs yell to every man, "RUN!" Actually, you must realize that with my lack of second dates, this has not proven to be my best approach. So, I have rethunk the whole strategy!

By the time most couples of my maturity are dating, their children have packed their bags and headed for the dorms. These older adults can, under candlelight and a leisurely dinner, sweetly reminisce about those lovely yummy teenage years. And, with their heads together, they can conspire about how their (simultaneous) roads could have been easier.

I, on the other hand, have just started on that path and will not be leaving CandyLand for some years to come. McDonald's playground and every sand-filled lot with a swing and monkey bars is a mainstay in my world. At all times, I have baby wipes somewhere on my body; lipstick is just another item to become smeared. Gray in the crayon box is now identified as the color before mommy colors her hair. My point is that candlelight is not just for ambiance; at my age, it is a necessity under lighting!

I, alone, have chosen this tough midlife motherhood road, which is actually more traveled these days by women electing to wait for children. So, a sense of humor and no complaints about the situation I have chosen for myself is my mantra-gait. For all of you neophyte midlife daters, here's a newsflash: our dates should expect the same as well. No moaning... well... not the bitching moans and groans... the other kind of (pleasurable) moaning in itself is truly worthy of another blog.

How I make this work is the simplest part of this equation. It is the same way I make it work for my children. I live in the moment and embrace the sheer delight of the sensation of the "now." It is that simple. I celebrate the wind in my face on the back of a motorcycle or the pure beauty of watching the sunset as I rollerblade and my date rides a bicycle. I just live in the moment of all situations that I want to fully embrace.

I am joyful to be a mom when I am with my children and joyful to be a woman when I am dating. If this realization in itself is the gift — the wisdom I have reaped

in my umber years — then rust-y just needs some WD-40
to let it rip.

On Failure, Forgiveness and Cutting Ourselves Some Slack

by Peg O'Neill, M.D.

We forgot about "Gotcha Day." In the world of adoptive families, this is a significant faux-pas. "Gotcha Day" is the celebration of bringing a non-biologic child into the family. For us, it commemorates the day our family became whole; the day that my husband and I were given the gift of our precious child and entered the challenging world of raising multiple boys, with all the craziness, motion, joy, and exhaustion. For my older son, it was the day he became a sibling and began his journey as a big brother. For my adoptive son, though he was just six months old when he joined our family forever, it is akin to a birthday — a momentous event, a beginning, a symbol of who he is, at least in part.

Over the past six years, we have commemorated "Gotcha Day" with story-telling about how we prayed for him to become part of our family, how we came to know him, and the details of how he joined our family, including how good he was on the plane coming back from Guatemala. We look at pictures, ooh and aah over how cute and funny he was. We go out to dinner at his favorite restaurant — a mediocre pasta joint near our house.

But this year, being the lousy parents that we sometimes are, we *forgot*. "Gotcha Day" arrived during a month when the craziness of our usual crazy lives was amplified ten-fold; a sudden staffing upheaval in my practice rendered me working more than usual; my pediatric boards, required every ten years with the stated goal of keeping clinicians current but really just designed to reduce even the most experienced doc to a pathetic pile of raw nerves, loomed. Throw in a little unexpected business travel for my husband, heaped on top of all the other usual stuff that, at baseline, requires herculean efforts to balance, and the perfect storm for forgetting something important was created. So, we sort of had a few good excuses for forgetting "Gotcha Day."

Tell that to a six-year old. My husband was the one who suddenly, the day after, remembered, announcing our transgression with an appropriate degree of horror and shame. Our son, who like most first-graders is more focused on his birthday and didn't even know the exact date of "Gotcha Day," immediately felt the sting of parental neglect. The fact that his older brother reminded him that he only had a birthday and didn't even have a "Gotcha Day" (in the score-keeping that siblings often engage, this has somehow rendered *him* a neglected child), did not help. There was a bit of indignation on the younger neglected child's end, and a lot of apologizing on our part. I felt horrible guilt, and wondered whether I forgot this year because of the unusually-large number of balls I was juggling, or simply because of a peri-menopausal memory lapse.

Whatever the reason, whatever the excuse, we screwed up. Caught up in the craziness of our work lives, we overlooked an important event in the part of our lives that is most precious to us — that of our family. We couldn't take it back. There was no opportunity to rewind. So we acknowledged our mistake, apologized, and moved on. Fortunately, we were forgiven. We rescheduled "Gotcha Day" to the following weekend, and we had a great time at the mediocre pasta joint. We told some stories about the beginning of our whole family, about the entrance of our nearly-toothless six year old into our lives when he was a tiny baby.

I'm pretty sure that this was a good "Gotcha Day." I'm pretty sure that my child will not require therapy down the road for this mistake, though I'm equally confident that we will be reminded of our lapse periodically by both of our kids.

Children love to remind their parents, who are supposed to be on the ball and run the show, of when they have epically failed. My pre-adolescent already has a small arsenal of zingers, which he chooses to pull out at various opportune moments: "Remember the time, Mom, when I was two and you closed the car door on my finger?" Or, "Remember the time, Mom, when I had a fever for a week and you told me I just had a virus and then you *finally* took me to the doctor and I had pneumonia?" And so on. Now my younger one has some ammunition, too.

This is probably not the first time we have erred, and it probably won't be the last. Though we try our best, we sometimes fail in our parenting duties. How we handle our failures can help teach our kids how to handle theirs. Admitting your mistake, asking forgiveness, moving on, and trying to do better the next time is what we ask of our children when they fail. We shouldn't expect less of ourselves.

Thru the Eyes of a Midlife Mother
by Shana Sureck

Everyone was having children. Except me. Co-workers. Friends. The teenagers I taught in an afterschool program. The moms at the mall who yanked at their children's arms and made them cry with curses and slaps.

I received birth announcements. Baby shower invites. I wanted to celebrate and feel joy for my friends, but each new announcement brought a yearning for what I couldn't have.

Year in and year out, at the Jewish High Holidays, as the Biblical story of Hannah was read, I cried as she wept and prayed silently for a child in such an impassioned way that the guard at the temple thought she was drunk.

As a newspaper photographer, I photographed children everywhere. I was famous for my happy, quirky kid pictures, like it was my informal niche. I loved them — their smiles, mischief, and innocence. The sweetness of their faces could take my breath away. Many of the page one photographs of children were mine.

I was in my early thirties in a marriage challenged by infertility, among other things. Despite a promise that he and I would have a child, and despite having been matched by our doctor with a donor who matched him in certain characteristics, he said no. He didn't think he had it in him to be a father again. The marriage went from challenged to stressed-at-the-seams. Years passed. Fibroids grew where a child didn't and I needed surgery to even keep the hope of a child alive.

At work, I was on fire. I threw myself into my photo assignments, learning about people, connecting to social issues, feeling the exhilaration of authentic visual storytelling. I loved making pictures, and the paper gave me the rare freedom to wander and explore with a camera, knowing I could be trusted to bring back stories that mattered to me and to readers.

One day, a student in an afterschool program I taught called to tell me his mother had been shot and killed while hanging laundry. I drove over. He was cradling a vase of fresh cut flowers from her garden, a beautiful bountiful garden on a block in Hartford better known for abandoned houses, drugs, and the shooting of an unarmed teenager. His tears poured out. These were the last flowers she would ever cut.

On that same day, a wealthy couple was found bludgeoned to death in a botched robbery less than a mile away in their home in the neighboring West Hartford. They were white. They were philanthropists. They commanded the attention of half a dozen reporters from the paper, two photographers, countless editors, and my student's mother, Edwina Reid, black, poor, unknown in an elite social milieu, didn't receive as much as a police brief.

Something hit home at that moment beyond the obvious — and appalling — racial (and class) bias. Who was deciding whose life was important and whose wasn't, and why? What made some people newsworthy and others not? There was a great pool of wonderful people doing amazing things in their lives who didn't have a voice, who weren't recognized. I went to the funeral of Mike's mother. 600 people packed the pews. Again, as in much of my work life, an incredible theme emerged. Rich, poor, black, white, Hispanic, we share dreams and hopes for ourselves and our children. We have pain that we learn from and overcome, and our differences are far less than what we have in common. I became less of an observer and more of a participant.

Through a column called "Rituals," which I then began writing and photographed, I held the spiritual hands of many who had known loss and pain but who nonetheless celebrated the love and life they had through rituals that exploded with meaning and beauty. My camera and keyboard recorded the stories of foster children, couples reaching 50 years of marriage, a woman in hospice care. When I wanted to take pictures for a ritual on bedtime stories, I went to the homeless shelter and found a young mom who read to her kids and wanted all the same things for her kids as any of us. I was in the company of many extraordinary ordinary people whose struggles and resilience resonated both with me and with readers.

I loved this work, I loved mentoring Hartford youth in an afterschool journalism program, and came to accept that maybe this, not being a parent, was what I was meant to do. I tried to move on.

When my marriage ended, I knew I had a small window to try once more. I was 39 and single. I also was alone and longing even more for motherhood. I chose a donor — Jewish, from Paris, a marathon runner and filmmaker — and on the fourth try I was pregnant. After she was born, I was blessed with an amazing community of friends who celebrated my pregnancy and wrapped my newborn and me in a loving embrace — quite literally with a handmade quilt, each square of which was designed by each friend.

In this new life, I photographed my daughter incessantly. Once I took a roll of film of her sleeping and asked for double prints. The lab guy was incredulous. What can I tell you? New parents are crazy, drunk with love for our little beings, and now I was part of that group.

I stopped taking many of the risks that go with being a photojournalist. When the paper told me I was being embedded with a US military unit in Iraq for two weeks, I just laughed. I passed on out-of-town trips. I drove more slowly getting to hostage situations, giving the cops more time to get the situation under control. I made myself invisible when they were looking to send someone to a gang shooting.

My column got a little schmaltzy and baby-centric, and was cancelled for being too spiritual. The personal pain and struggle of my childlessness made for good writing. The awe and wonder of new parenthood did not. I quit my full-time job, but I became more passionate than ever about my work, my life, and my heart.

Here are my thoughts: we need photographs and stories more than ever, stories that look beyond our differences to the hearts that beat the same, the dreams that we cherish but that can be so easily extinguished without nurture and acknowledgment, but a new model for telling them is yet to emerge.

I still cringe when I walk by a mother yanking the arm of her child in the mall. In my work as a photographer, I've seen all too well what happens when kids aren't loved and understood. Although I'm no longer in the world as (my old self) a true newspaper photographer, I still look through the lens with the same awe and wonder, the same love.

On many weekends now, I'm photographing —

among other things - the bar and bat mitzvah of my daughter's peers. I can't help but cry at every one. I always loved the crazy, emerging spirit of teenagers, but it's a mother's appreciation I now bring to the sacred ritual and the beauty of generations connecting. While it's not breaking news, it's personal history unfolding, and I just don't click the button. I connect with my whole heart, catching the fleeting moments that celebrate love and life and make us whole.

Milky Magic: Thoughts on Breastfeeding from a Geriatric Mother

by Ellie Stoneley

I'm old. In nine months I'll be 50. I'm a first-time mother. I have a 22-month-old daughter. I drive along singing, "The Wheels on the Bus" even when she's not in the car with me. I secretly love it when she wakes up needing me in the night, however tired I am. I am still breastfeeding her.

So, it would appear that, certainly according to much of the tabloid press, I'm practically the devil incarnate. A crazy, breastfeeding, sagging old loon that a poor child has to put up with as a mother; a veritable harridan.

Personally I don't think I'm that bad.

I've surprised myself by taking to motherhood with a joy and zeal I never really imagined. For me, it's not just about being a mother, and being the best mother I possibly can be, it's also about mothering. About love and about nurture... and for me, that is where the breastfeeding comes in.

When Hope was first born, she was blue and "grunting." The sweet sound she was making wasn't sweet at all, it was the sound of her lungs failing; she was a poorly baby. She was taken off to the Special Care Baby Unit and came back to me with a tiny tube up her nose and an oxygen mask. I was told to express my milk, "liquid gold," precious colostrums, to put into the tube and into my girl. I found it so, so hard. Manual expressing was a total disaster for me. I managed less than a thimbleful that night. Maybe because of my aged breasts, or, due, perhaps, to the fact that she was almost a month early and delivered by Cesarean section. Who knows.

I struggled. I wept bitter, frustrated, exhausted tears as I tried to encourage her to fit her tiny mouth around my seeming huge nipples; to suckle, to nurse like all new born babies are supposed to do. I tried so many different holds. I recited over and over again "nose to nipple," "tummy to Mummy," and I felt endlessly disheartened as I sat with the gently sighing double breast pump trying to extract its illusive elixir.

I continued to battle with breastfeeding. During those early days I did frequently give her formula milk through the little nose tube when I didn't have the energy to pump, or tried and failed to get more than a teaspoonful of milk, or just couldn't manage getting her to feed from me. The midwife suggested her tongue might be tied; the consultant confirmed it - the tie was snipped and after that suckling grew easier. Then, she pulled out her feeding tube, which was very distressing (and long). It was reinserted but she pulled it out again and again.

The sixth time they decided not to put it back in and it was down to me to sustain my daughter. Over time, and with the help of the incredible ladies from the La Leche League, our confidence and ability grew, and the balance shifted to mainly breastfeeding with top ups of formula, or expressed milk which eventually started to flow. Other people enjoyed bottle feeding her — grandmothers, her father, aunts, and friends.

Then, on the day of her christening, when she was four months old, she suddenly stopped drinking from a bottle. That was it, she went 'cold turkey;' she just pushed the bottle away. From then on, it was just the two of us — me and Hope, Hope and me. Quiet intimate times and me, selfishly, proudly, reveling in the fact that I could sustain her entirely, myself. She refused all bottles until she was almost a year old, even after she'd started eating solid food.

As Hope started to become more agile, she would clamber over me and giggle as she latched on. Breastfeeding becomes a time when you are in a bubble with your small person; the world recedes and the elemental feeling of life nurturing life is so powerful. I am so lucky we've been able to feed at all. Especially with me being so old. In new mother terms, I'm considered positively "geriatric."

Nobody has ever commented when I've fed her in public. Only a close family member and friend made observations about the fact that we're still breastfeeding, at nearly two. "Are you going to be one of *those* women... like on the cover of Time magazine?" they asked. The answer was a resounding, "I hope so." Especially, if that's what Hope wants and it's still right for both of us. Being over 50 and breastfeeding? Shock and awe!

There we are. Not only did I manage, by a series of utter miracles and against all the odds, to have a child — a beautiful, happy perfect baby girl — but, I have been able to breastfeed her. It was hard work to begin with, but we persevered and relish every minute. Long may it continue.

This very contented older mother, is about to go to bed after a day singing about sleeping bunnies, scarecrows, and black sheep. I'm looking forward to being awakened bright and early by a hungry chatty little girl who will call out to me, "Mummy, milky, Mummy," and will then nuzzle in to feast, and break off with milk

running down her chin, and say, "Yummy."
  Now then, where are my bedsocks?

A Child of My Own
by Michelle Eisler

I was walking through an antique store when a lady approached me to say how adorable my daughter was, and that now that I had adopted I would get pregnant and have a child of my "own." I had not met her, spoken to her about my road to adoption, nor about infertility and whether it played a role in my world. But she continued to tell me her friend had finally given up and adopted, and then she got pregnant.

Many (most) adoptive parents experience things similar to my encounter. "Do you have any of your *own*? Do you plan to have your *own* child?" I could brush it away as "another woman had this child" …but really that isn't what is being asked of me. They mean biologically, thus resulting in the child officially being mine.

Others may think I am being picky about wording, or obsessing about semantics. Clearly my daughter is adopted — I am white and she is brown. Obviously, the woman is just chatting me up, telling me a story about her friend. When strangers ask questions, it usually isn't with the intent to be rude.

I remember, as a child, having various children introduced to me as someone's "adopted" child. Each time, it didn't matter what ethnicity they were, the significance was that they were adopted.

If you are following what I have said, so far, you are noticing that everything is from an adult's perspective.

But, now think if my daughter was older and capable of understanding the statement "a child of my own." The children I was introduced to (so long ago) as "adopted" were around eight years old at the time. What kind of impact did these statements have on them?

I do not want to see what will happen to me if I hear the words "adopted daughter" always prefacing my child's name. I think the same knife which could pierce her heart will also pierce mine. I share who she is with her Haitian Mother; she carries her blood and her characteristics. But this little girl carries both of our hearts.

I have loved her since my eyes first saw her wrinkly little face and her tiny knit hat. I fought for her when I thought I had lost her because of an unexpected tragedy in her birth country. I cannot put all the different emotions I felt into words, describing the first time I held her. I have been up with her while she cried, been to the hospital with her when she was sick, and had anxiety attacks stressing over things that will likely never happen.

To throw an extra word in front of son/daughter removes a portion of the bond any child has to their family. If there are biological siblings involved, it makes for an even more damaging situation — it creates an opening for a child to feel "less-than." This girl in question is my daughter. My daughter by way of adoption, and yes, it is just semantics, but the wording does not preface my child's identity within my family.

I used to feel that I needed to share details about our adoption experience so that people wouldn't judge our family and the extended family in Haiti. I have since come to understand the necessity for a cloak of protection that families chose to shield their adopted children's story. I am thankful my daughter arrived here as a baby and didn't hear me blathering on. Now, I am the only one carrying this shame.

Much of who our children are is tied to their story; we, as the next bearers, should only be adding to it, not taking away. These children have already experienced too much loss before they come to be our sons and daughters. We can never afford to give away more of who they are.

If you are in a position where you must introduce someone's adopted child(ren), introduce him or her by his or her name, only. If you see a family who looks like mine, refrain from asking personal things. People will always have questions, it is inherent in human nature. However, a child's history is not your story.

Giving Birth to Life and Death
by Amy Wright Glenn

My 18-month-old son blissfully naps and I decide to catch up on some emails. I look at my inbox and notice a request for advice. I open the email, curious. After reading the first sentence, I take a deep breath.

"I experienced my first stillborn birth as a doula. I am so confused."

The new doula in question had witnessed one of life's most painful experiences — the birth of a lifeless infant.

"I did my best to support these new parents experiencing such a sudden and tragic blow to their expectant hearts," she continued. "But now, they've asked me to speak at the funeral. What can I say?"

Her grief, concern, and confusion touch me. I pause and close my eyes. How to respond to her request? I'm flooded with memories.

Having worked as a hospital chaplain, I've witnessed very painful episodes in life. From holding the shaking body of a mother whose son committed suicide, to placing my hand on the lifeless chest of a murdered man, I know what it is like to cry and pray with strangers. Having looked at the still face of death, I breathe in wonder and bow to the mystery that awaits us all. As a chaplain, I needed to breathe particularly mindfully while supporting parents through the bewildering grief of losing a baby.

I close my eyes and meditate. Silent tears accompany my response. I type a meditation for her to share with those who will gather in sorrow. I encourage her to weave her own words into the fabric of my own.

Please join me in the spirit of meditation. Place your hands on your lap. Place your feet on the steady earth. Close your eyes as inspired. Soften the muscles of your face. Let your breath begin to move through tight places.

May the breath you take right now be a reminder of life's precious fragility.

May the inhale give strength at this difficult time.

May the exhale create space for the natural stages of grief.

We meditate with a spirit of the open heart. We meditate and remember the dead.

We meditate and remember this precious and beloved child.

Birth and death are mysteries.

We place these mysteries in our hearts and bow to the power of a love that transcends the understanding of any human mind.

I place my hands on the keyboard and complete my email to the heartsick doula. I urge her to take what works and leave the rest.

"Trust your heart," I write.

Later that night, I watch my son sleep beside me. Witnessing his beauty transports me with grace. Yet, sadness accompanies this gratitude. He and I share a common destiny with all that live. Through my body, my son entered this human world. Because of this fact, one day he will die. I have no idea when and how my son will move through death's doorway, but I do know that door will open. It's an irrevocable and unalterable truth. No one receives an immortal human experience.

All that lives in time and space must die in time and

space. I imagine there is a light that breathes into this dance and transcends it. I trust that this light is made of inexhaustible love.

I continue to watch him sleep. A green, handmade quilt rests over us. It was crafted with love by my paternal grandmother. My son never met his great-grandmother in this life. Will he ever know the woman whose hands stitched together this beautiful gift with profound love? Did they meet before he came to me? Will I ever see her again?

My mind can pose a million philosophical questions but nothing brings me peace until my heart relaxes into the mystery. I feel most alive when trusting that soft, gentle kindness within. May I pierce the everyday chatter of my to-do list with a mindfulness of the sacred essence manifesting in each moment. May I surrender with grace to time's relentless dance.

Jalaluddin Rumi, the famous 13th century Muslim mystic wrote, "Whoever knoweth the dance, dwelleth in God."

May you know the dance.

Infertile, me? No way — I'm Latina
by Liz Raptis Picco

I'm 60, raising teenage brothers who my husband and I adopted from Ciudad Juárez, Chihuahua, almost fifteen years ago. Being a Latina and native speaker definitely helped when we approached an orphanage in northern Mexico. Being a Latina also made it difficult for me to talk about it openly among my family.

I've noticed the same reluctance in Latinas to discuss infertility and IVF, as well as adoption. I follow many wonderful blogs where important issues concerning Latinas are showcased, but I have not yet found one that discusses infertility.

Why?

Because infertility tends to shame and isolate women who ultimately end up suffering in silence, believing they are the only ones. I did.

For years I struggled to get pregnant, believing it was only a matter of time before I joined that coveted inner circle of womanhood. Infertile. Me? No way, I'm Latina. I'd bought into the myth of our universal fertility.

I grew up as one of eleven siblings in southwestern Arizona where it seemed I was related to half the population on both sides of the border. Mexican mother, Greek father: how could I possibly be infertile?

I remember my maternal grandmother, Nachu, rejecting the notion that I would be childless after years of painful disappointment. In her faintly perfumed bedroom, she gave me a San Judas novena, blessed me with her warm plump hand, and said, "no one in this family is infertile." She cupped my chin, trained her eyes on mine, and said that I was merely a late bloomer.

I desperately wanted to believe her. I took that novena and her loving promise, and I hid my pain. I girded myself at countless baby showers and baptisms where someone would inevitably ask if I had any children. Piercing sadness and awkwardness would replace the small talk. I'd turn away or bolt to the bathroom and cry.

Infertility sucks, plain and simple. For me, it sucked even more because I took it on alone, except for my husband. No one discussed it. In my family's case, they didn't want to hurt my feelings or were afraid they'd jinx my chances. We are a superstitious lot. But after three, five, and then ten years not having children, I needed my family to fill my empty arms.

Twenty-five years later, I still sense the same squirming discomfort among my family when we discuss someone who is having trouble conceiving. The air seems tainted by embarrassment as the conversation drifts away, heads shaking in empathy. No one uses the word infertile. Instead they say that the problem is nothing more than bad luck, the evil eye, or the fact that the unfortunate woman works too much.

I'm reminded of the time when I uttered the forbidden word around a tableful of women, and my mother cupped her hand over mine and shot me a silent reproach. Later she explained it was rude, no different than talking about one's sex life in mixed company.

Is it rude to bring up or is it rude to avoid it?

All Done

by Andrea Hopkins

I've done it. I've put the baby gear up for sale. The Bjorn. The exersaucer. The infant car seat and the Bumbo chair. Taken photos, written reassuringly about a pet-free and smoke-free home, and hit "post ad." The pile of gear, cleaned up for the photo op, now sits in the middle of the dining room awaiting eager buyers, ignored by the three year old, and used only as a hand-hold by the baby, who toddles by haltingly on the way to her next task, oblivious to the detritus of her infancy.

I think I'm done. I've still got frozen embryos from the last round of IVF, but I've got two happy kids, 33 years left on the mortgage, a constant contented fatigue and a rapidly graying head of hair. Two children are probably enough. Our little family of three feels about right.

But. There is a lingering longing. Could I have had a third child, if I were richer? Married? Younger? And what if I change my mind? How long can I possibly wait before knowing my decision to have two, and only two, is final? Can I wait until the kids are in school, when I have a chance to catch my breath, before finally deciding about a third? With frozen embryos, the clock's ticking is slightly subdued. The snooze button pushed, as it were. But too old is too old, frozen embryos or not. Am I there yet?

The question isn't just about me. One of my closest friends, 49, is trying to have a second child. Her firstborn, like mine, is three. He was conceived with her own eggs when she was 46, through IVF. Like me, she is a Single

Mother by Choice.

We each reached middle age alone, but determined to be a mother. Without a partner, we each turned to an anonymous sperm donor and a fertility clinic to conceive, and we each became overjoyed, contented, confident single mothers.

She drove me home from my second IVF egg retrieval, the day Anna was conceived in a Petri dish. She blames my easy experience with IVF for sparking her desire for a second child. Since then, she has undergone another IVF, but without luck. Now she is considering donor eggs or embryos, comfortable with the notion of building her family in whatever way she can. Her own mother is not as comfortable. She worries about her daughter's age and her stamina, though my friend is as fit and active, healthy and serene, wise, and funny as anyone we know.

Age is subjective. Mental. Emotional. As young as you feel, as old as you fear. But age is also biological, and if being pregnant at 40 or 45 or 50 isn't daunting enough, attending a high school graduation ceremony at 70 is. And age is financial. Last week I finally crossed the last thing off my post-partum to-do list: I opened college savings accounts for the girls. One each, a nominal amount deposited monthly, investments chosen for their moderate risk. Saving for college, at the expense of saving for retirement. I can't do both right now, not with the childcare expenses and the mortgage and the life insurance premiums and the, you know, food and diapers.

Suze Orman would disapprove — she favors retirement savings over college savings, since you can borrow for college but not for retirement. But I have a company pension (so far), existing retirement savings, and a steadily appreciating house in a city where there is never a housing slump. Still, the finances of midlife mothering are daunting. My own parents retired young, in their fifties, house paid off, kids done college. Starting motherhood late means I may well have to work past 65 to meet all our goals, to hang onto the family home even when it is an empty nest, to have enough money to help my parents, if they need it, or my girls, when they do.

But more than the finances, closing the door on more children is a stark statement of age. I like being a new mom, able to talk about pregnancy or breast pumps or sleep training, the merits of a particular kind of stroller or diaper, the folly of food mills and baby sunglasses. I'm not yet so far removed from it that I have to say, "Oh, when mine were little, we did this..." or "The guidelines have changed since then, but we always..." I can still describe baby poop without batting an eye. Once I move on, I leave that club of new mothers that I waited so long to join.

My friends with 10 year olds tell me they don't even remember these baby days, sometimes. They can't quite recall what was so endearing about their baby's drool or their toddler's screech. They have no idea what they did all day with these tiny people — their lives are now about Xboxes and preteen angst. I'm not sure I'm ready to leave the baby club. Now that Anna is walking, officially a toddler, I see moms with new babies, tiny newborns, and feel a twinge of jealousy. Am I really past that? Have I really left that behind, forever?

Well, probably. I probably have. Looking on the bright side, everyone in my house sleeps through the night, holds their own spoon, and climbs the stairs on their own. I still bear the brunt of dishwashing and teeth brushing, but I have big plans to delegate on both of those fronts within the next few years. Maybe I am ready to move on, too.

In the meantime, I take photos of every age and stage, knowing how fleeting all of it is. And I sort the baby gear, and sell off my old favorites. Because having one January baby and one June means the hand-me-downs are off by a season, and the footwear dilemma is getting ugly. Baby needs new shoes. C'mon Craig's List. Baby needs new shoes. And when she's done with them, I'll box them up with the keepsakes, because we won't be needing to hand them down to anyone.

The Wilderness of Motherhood

by Lora Freeman Williams

A pregnancy test is like a Rorschach: one's inner world gets tossed back at her in sharp relief. I stared at mine and felt the weight of my childhood and the hope of a different future in a dizzying twist of emotions.

My own mother had become pregnant with me in 1968, when she was single and an as yet undiagnosed schizophrenic. Exhibiting a striking combination of paranoia and common sense, she moved herself and me a few hundred miles away from her dysfunctional relations and embarked on the next 13 years of our life together.

She never held a job for long, and in most of the years we lived together, she prostituted to provide us food and shelter, neither of which we had predictably or steadily. My mom was intelligent, beautiful, capable of moments of tenderness and good humor, and these very significant contributions to my childhood probably saved me from insanity despite the traumas. In 1981, the State of Wisconsin intervened, the bruises and scratches on my face and neck and arms from my mother's latest attack too obvious to others for them to ignore, and I entered foster care for the remainder of my teens.

And at 37, I was newly pregnant, single and panicked. It was quite clear to me that despite lots of therapy and spiritual practices, I wasn't yet a very good parent to myself. I was still searching for my calling in life and hoping to make more money and get out of debt and finally get into a healthy romantic relationship. I didn't want to be a single parent. But I felt the bond with my mustard seed of a baby already, my body raging with hormonal urges to cocoon my child and protect him from harm. A spark of hope arose within me with this new spark of life: perhaps the Universe had given me a personal invitation to the fast track of healing?

Like addicts sent to wilderness therapy for the summer, maybe I was on the edge of the wilderness of motherhood, where I would learn greater character and will and strength and wholeness than my previous life had taught me? Maybe my greater freedoms in singleness were not so great; maybe greater freedom felt a lot like being lost. I was intrigued with what the wilderness time might hold, intrigued with what it might make of me.

So I got myself in gear and prepared for a new life that started the moment he was born. I managed to condense all of my work into tasks I could do from home, so that when my sweet child slept, I could rush to the computer to make our living. I moved in with friends who had children so I could watch others parents and learn from them, and I could also keep our expenses down. And I got really, really tired.

My own spark got low. I loved my little boy before he was born, and I loved him more when I held him and stayed up awake with him at night and when I wanted to nap with him during the day and couldn't. And it took everything out of me to love him and to work while he slept. I got very lonely. I couldn't run around my old haunts in Chicago looking for social situations where I might get hugs or have a deep conversation that would sustain my need to be loved and seen. I abandoned my New Age Church, where I got nothing but flakey platitudes. I went on a few dates, but they clearly sucked on my limited energy, and I dropped them, too. I withdrew because I had to. I had to conserve what little I had in order to keep our little family boat afloat.

And a shift started to happen.

One of the deepest wounds of my childhood had been that I learned I did not matter. My hungers and desires were a burden to my mother who could barely feed and shelter me. My noise disrupted her already scattered thoughts. My observations didn't fit with her twisted ones, and she told me I was wrong. And so, in order to survive, I had agreed with her. I hid my hungers from even myself; I became quiet to avoid disturbing anyone; I kept my thoughts to myself because exposing them just exposed me to ridicule.

And in this very early time of Isaac's life, my little spark of life got so low and small and so critically essential to my child's well-being, that I began to protect and nurture it. I took my precious little time alone to write an essay or two about what I was learning. I started to notice that some people actually gave me more energy than they took, and I sought them out.

I learned that sucking up the happy moments of my life was a balm that healed the wounds of my youth, and I allowed myself the freedom to do that. I learned to pay attention, even in the inevitable miserable moments of parenting, because my presence with myself and with my son fed us both. I learned that I could be kind and compassionate to both my son and to myself in the middle of the pains of life, and one step at a time along the path, I practiced doing that.

This little boy whose profile looks so much like my own when I was young has healed me. He has taught me that in loving him well and fully, I must love myself, too. This wild adventure in uncharted territory gave me what

I'd hoped for.

I am 45 years old as I write this. My son is seven and a half. We live in more civilized and sheltered times, but we would not be where we are now were it not for the time we'd spent in the wilderness together.

An Introverted Mother
by Denise Naus

Being an introvert and a mother of three seem to be at odds with each other. As an introvert, I tend to crave quiet and ALONE perhaps more than my extroverted human counterparts might. And yet my young children are constantly here... and there... and... everywhere!

This is my fantasy "happy place" in my mind: I am alone in the forest. Alone in the cabin — miles from any civilization. It's only me and the woodland creatures. The songs of birds, the calls of the wolves, and the occasional growl of a bear. There is no Internet. No telephone. But there are books (many books)! There is pen and paper. And God.

And, I am blissfully happy.

At least, that is what I imagine I would feel. This is a place I imagine my introverted-self running to when life becomes too full... of people, activities, and demands.

Despite all this, I home-educate my children. This has proven to have many benefits and blessings. But I confess that some days the big yellow school bus also enters my fantasy world and whispers to me, "Let me take away your children." Ahhh, this idea that all my children disappear for a few hours each day. Time when I could exact order and cleanliness on my home, and no interruptions on my reading time. Of course, reality rarely works that way.

Does every mother dream at times of running away? Of course. But not everyone needs this escape to the same level of intensity. Susan Cain, author of **Quiet: The Power of Introverts In a World That Can't Stop Talking,** speaks about how introversion is not acceptable in a society which values group interaction. She writes, "...solitude matters. And, in fact, for some people — it is the air they breathe."

Is this why I often feel so short of breath?

A short while ago, my sister and I were daydreaming about getting away on a holiday — away from our kids, husbands, and all our many responsibilities. I asked her how long could she go before she would miss her children? Her response — a day or two. I laughed. That's barely enough time to catch my breath! I could leave for a week, I'm sure. And that causes me to feel some guilt. Am I a less loving mother because of this?

As an introvert, I feel as though there is this constant battle inside of me. I want to run away and be alone, but I love my children and often want to be around them. I crave silence, but want to enjoy their play, even if it is louder than my senses can comfortably handle. I crave peace, but their bickering and fighting are like 100 nails on a chalkboard. Some days, I confess, I just want to cover my ears and run away. I covet time to read books uninterrupted. Lots and lots of books. Books I used to stay up until 4 a.m. reading because... well, because I could. Because no job I have ever had has demanded as much of me as these children do.

But does this make me less of a mother? According to many parenting books, yes. Because I should enjoy sitting down to play with them, right? I really don't. I should love taking them out on outings to experience life all the time, right? But, I like to stay home. Does this make me less of a mother? No, it does not.

There are gifts I can give to my children that might

only be best taught by an introvert. For instance, I could teach them how to enjoy their own company. Even extroverts need time to just be alone, and hopefully learn how to take pleasure in that — if only for short periods of time.

My very outgoing five year old must take a one- hour quiet-time every day. Now, she is learning what to do during that time that she enjoys — on her own. She will listen to radio theatre, read books and listen to music. She doesn't love to be alone and would still prefer her little sister there — but I see her coming out of her room more centered, more at peace with herself. It makes me wonder: If we can't enjoy quiet time on our own, how many opportunities to hear (from) God might we be missing?

Hopefully, we can come to accept and love our own introverted selves enough to pass along this acceptance to our children no matter where they lie on the introverted/extroverted scale, so that they can see the value of each human being as God created them. We each have something valuable to give each other. I have very extroverted friends who tell me that they have learned that it's ok to slow down and say "no" more often just by being my friend. In return, they teach me how to not take myself so seriously and enjoy life.

According to Susan Cain, "The more freedom we give introverts to be themselves, the more likely they are to come up with unique solutions to problems." I have not had enough time to be myself to figure out how to make this cabin in the woods a reality. But, maybe if I can listen to my own voice calling me away to quiet time, even in small spaces throughout my day, the call of the quiet in the woods won't be quite so strong.

Bat Mitzvah Revisited
by Randi Hoffman

Sitting at my computer in my bedroom I can hear an old man screaming at my daughter. He says, "Get back here! You are being very disrespectful!" She is sitting at her father's desk in the living room, crying and staring at the ground. The normally cordial and gentle rabbi is on Skype attempting to go over her Torah portion with her. She had gone on a quest searching the apartment for Wite Out (to fix a wrong Hebrew vowel) without informing him, leaving him looking at an empty chair. This is not a good situation, and I have a feeling it will end badly.

My 12-year-old daughter's Bat Mitzvah is coming up in a few months. For the most part, I don't mind planning the event. It's a lot of work, and I wouldn't want to plan events for a living, but I can do it. I can set up all the moving pieces. I've arranged the religious service, DJ party, and lunch at an atmospheric factory converted into a restaurant in Williamsburg, Brooklyn. Far removed from the deli platter back at the house that marked my own coming of age.

I have vivid memories of my own tempestuous adolescence, so now it is my turn to nurture a moody, spirited girl. As a quiet, serious, bookish kid, I wanted an existential, meaningful reason to believe in Judaism. I had some friends, but I wasn't that social at 13, so, the justification of "You'll have a party with all your friends! You'll get presents!" didn't cut it with me. My daughter, however, is interested in inviting a horde of teenagers and is balking at the absence of a photo booth.

I remember 12 as a painful, awkward age. I was not comfortable in my new body yet, and I felt ugly. I was very skinny, tall and gangly, and I had acne. My daughter is more at ease, more graceful, and more stylish (although the low-cut bellbottoms dragging behind me signify a grungier era). Or maybe this is just a perception from the other side. She is an athlete on the track team, running 400 meter and one mile races with ease.

But, while I didn't have to think twice about going to the area high school in ninth grade, my daughter has the added pressure of competing to get into one of NYC's top high schools during this same time period. She knows she is smart and hardworking, but not a dazzling math wizard, so the whole process is very stressful for her. Simultaneous to her Bat Mitzvah preparations, she is taking a labor-intensive test prep course. I pushed the Bat Mitzvah back a few months after her birthday so the two events would not completely overlap; but still, having to do the work for both huge milestones in the same season is putting her over the edge.

I did not grow up in an observant household. My parents sent me to Hebrew school at a Reform congregation in a leafy suburb, with many of my schoolmates. The main thrust of the curriculum was remembrance of the Holocaust. We were shown *Night and Fog*, a documentary about the death camps: featuring lampshades made of Jewish skin. We were taught that if you scratched the surface, most non-Jews were anti-Semitic, proven by the Nazis. Israel was the Promised Land - the one place on Earth where we are the majority, where no one could persecute or deport us. Anyone criticizing anything at all about Israel or its political policies was branded anti-Semitic.

This congregation was presided over by a playful, joking rabbi, who liked to walk around saying, "Have you seen the rabbi?" When I told my mother he seemed like a fool and I wanted to learn more about Judaism, she said, "No, he's not a scholar. But he's a nice guy. He's not arrogant like other rabbis."

I picked our current congregation after attending High Holiday services for Rosh Hashanah and Yom Kippur in a barely renovated 19th century cathedral of a synagogue on the Lower East Side of Manhattan. I loved the talented band playing both classical and Klezmer music, and the familiar ancient prayers. And while this rabbi has crossed the line into New Age thinking and lapsed into talk about angels, he is welcoming to non-Jews, of which my husband is one. Forty years later, the wound of the Holocaust has lessened, and it is possible to criticize Israeli policy without being branded a traitor. The Hebrew school stresses joy, not suspicion and paranoia, and there is a weekly service of Israeli and Jewish music, and classes full of discussion. This congregation has no permanent building of its own, hence no building fund, and the Hebrew school has met in yoga and dance and drama studios, with Friday night services at a Quaker meeting house.

I had hoped that this journey with my daughter would be inspiring and spiritual for both of us, a connection to our ancient heritage. The reality is an exercise in motivating a kid to do what she doesn't want to do, and attempting to help her organize and structure her studying time. I've given up trying to find a spark of illumination or meaning for her.

We've broken down what she needs to learn into parts, and are trying to tackle each part. After one horribly upsetting phone call with the rabbi, some emails back and forth and a family meeting, we are more or less back on track. She has begun Skyping with the rabbi again. I would not say she is joyful about it, but she is resigned to her fate, and more diligent. The experience has not brought out the best in either of us. But I am still holding out hope that there will be a magical spiritual moment on the day of the ceremony that will make it all worth it.

My Journey into Midlife Motherhood
by Karen C. Hug-Nagy

Becoming a first-time Mom of twins at age forty-five was like viewing a meteor shower! Within an instant, I could sense a *shift* coming my way. I suspected something was about to change, and it did, with a loud BANG! Raising kids is comparable to jumping from one orbit to the next.

The definition of an orbit:

"The path described by a heavenly body in its periodical revolution around another body; as, the orbit of Jupiter, of the earth, of the moon." www.brainquote.com.

So how do I operate in this midlife Mom orbit? I orbit my kids like the earth orbits the sun and the moon orbits the Earth. I nurture them, love them, and sometimes hover above them, like the stars.

Midlife motherhood has been a gift and a jolt into reality. How would I figure it all out? What were kids up to these days? How would I keep up with the younger Moms? Would people think I was Grandma instead of Mom?

Year by year, my questions were answered. I'm now more confident as a midlife mother. Many of the younger Moms were helpful in teaching me about the stages kids go through. I'm now tuned in to what kids are doing at school and with their friends. And yes, people ask me if I'm *the* Grandma, to which I promptly reply, "Nope, I'm their Mom!" Here we are, thirteen years later and entering the teen years. I call this the *chaotic orbit!* It's full of various types of space explosions! Lately, we have experienced what is called a *supernova* in astronomy terms. This happens when teen twins of the opposite sex agree to disagree on most every subject under the sun! These types of explosions can change life as we know it, disrupting an entire star while forming a *black hole.*

Mothering in midlife is a challenge, but as you well know, worth every moment you get to spend with your kids. It doesn't matter how many orbits we have to get through, or how long we wait for the next lunar eclipse. What matters is our love for our children and how miraculously they came to us.

The Chicken Back Syndrome

by Ann Sheybani

When did we women decide that everyone else should come first? Who proclaimed it our job to guarantee the pleasure of others and settle for whatever crumbs fall off their plates?

I've come to call this compulsion the Chicken Back Syndrome: preparing a chicken dinner, encouraging our husbands and children to take the best pieces — the breast, thighs and legs — and insisting that we actually like the chicken back best. Somehow, without question, everyone believes we're just crazy enough to prefer bones and gristle. After awhile, we even convince ourselves that those tiny scraps of meat buried between the ribs are worth the effort.

By reaching for the chicken back all the time we women train ourselves to ignore our own desires. At the same time, we teach those around us that we don't matter, that our satisfaction comes solely from seeing the people that we love enjoy the spoils.

This was a lesson I learned very early on at the knee of my mother: it was poor form to "put someone else out" by insisting on what I really wanted. I believed that nice girls reached for the smallest piece, or took what was offered them, and kept their yaps shut. Food, space, attention, it didn't matter which.

When my children were little they had no sense that I existed separate and apart from them, especially after their father and I got divorced. My world revolved around caring for them. There were no boundaries, no closed doors. They slept in my bed until they were practically 37. They argued with me while I sat on the toilet. They ruled the TV, and the weekend agenda. Nag me long enough, and I would drop what I was doing to satisfy their whims. When I refused them their wishes in favor of my own, they smelled my guilt, and took advantage of it. Such is the nature of that beast.

Like my mother before me, I had come to believe that if I went along with what everybody else wanted, if I sacrificed in the name of being a good wife or mother, if I denied that I had a preference, if I put away my desires like an old sewing project, then I would earn my family's undying love. Truth be told, I didn't believe I was lovable simply for being the woman that I was.

Instead of reaping affection, here's what happened:

- I learned that teenagers and undying love don't actually go together in the same sentence.
- My kids developed a sense of entitlement that won't serve them well in the world.
- I became resentful and anxious because I'd relinquished control.
- I gained a lot of weight because, with no room for romance, I made love to cake.

So, it's no wonder I forgot who I was and what I wanted after a few years of that. It was hard to remember I liked breast meat after eating chicken back.

Eventually I decided that, as a woman, it was never going to be my turn, unless I TOOK it. I realized that a middle-aged, overweight, anxious, resentful, passive aggressive mama with no life just isn't sexy.

So, for some reason I no longer remember, I went off on a solitary bike trip to the heart of France. I met fabulous people, couples who'd been married forever and were still mutually enthralled. Inspired, I came home with a vision of a life I knew I could love, and I screwed up the courage to go after my desires. Believe me when I say, I faced plenty of guff.

Little by little, I began to invest in myself, pamper myself, because somehow I sensed that no one would love me until I could. That's how I met and married a man who treats me like a goddess, and in the process, learned how to RECEIVE, not just give.

There are a few expressions I've run into a lot lately, geared mostly to business, but completely applicable to what we're talking about here:

1. People will only be willing to invest in you to the degree that you're willing to invest in yourself.
2. You don't get what you're worth; you get what you negotiate.

Negotiate the small things, and the big things will follow.

And tonight? Place the chicken breast on your plate, and the leg, then eat the whole damned thing. It's your job to teach your kids that other people — particularly you — matter.

A woman who takes care of herself first, who recognizes that no one is happy if mama ain't happy, is sexy as hell.

Down Syndrome Awareness - Can We Have Some Dignity to Go With That?

A Commentary by Laura Sussely - Pope

The month of October, Down syndrome month, is a particularly good time to bring awareness to the fact that the "r" word (retard) is exceedingly hurtful. For those who don't realize how hurtful it is, many of us point it out as nicely as we can. And, if we are lucky, the offending party apologizes and tries not to do it again. We are not, for the most part, an unforgiving bunch. We recognize that most people use it with no malice or forethought. In daily conversation, it has become a synonym for "stupid" or "silly" or "ridiculous."

The first time I worried about this word was nine years ago when my son was born. As I sat numb, in shock, and listening to the geneticist explaining his Down syndrome diagnosis, I interrupted and cried, "I just don't want anyone calling him a retard!" Little did I know just how likely this was to happen.

But what about the many who *do* know better and continue using it? The use of the word has increased as social media and the Internet have grown. One popular site offers a quiz that asks, "How Retarded Are You?" I don't know the answer, but if my nine-year-old son could read, write or talk, I would ask him. Another application on the same site offers another quiz allowing members to "see what famous retard" they are most like.

As an administrator on many online parenting sites,

not one day passes that I don't see this word freely being used, most surprisingly by mothers who may one day have a child with Down syndrome (or another related condition) which may cause their child to be called a "retard."

Many subscribers defend their use of the word and insist on being allowed to use it even when the pain it causes is clearly pointed out to them.

The prevalence of "retard" on the web is astronomical. If you look at the Special Olympics Spread the Word to End the Word site, there is a widget one can use to see how many times in one day the "r" word is used on any given website. It is eye-opening. All you really have to do is Google the word and let the counting begin...

Want to hear it over and over again? Turn on the TV. I like TV, but if I were to go one week without hearing a character use this word, I'd be shocked. Name a sitcom or reality show, and there is a good chance it will be said. While the media may publicize the more blatant and obvious attacks on children like mine, this is surely the tip of the iceberg.

As I marvel at how hard my little guy works to do what comes easily for those who casually say, "I'm so retarded," all I can think to reply is, "No, you're not, but my son is." This brings me to the next point. He can't defend himself — which is what makes all of this more hateful than ever.

On the "Spread the Word" Facebook group, someone once wrote that our kids should simply grow thick skins and defend themselves. If my child had the mental capacity and ability to talk, it might be possible, but what part of my saying, "He can't," does that person not understand?

Sadly, I've come to expect these hurtful and thoughtless statements from strangers, acquaintances and friends. I've come to expect the "r" word to be tossed around, defended and downplayed on a regular basis. But, please note that we also hear it from loved ones and those we truly respect.

Sticks and stones may break my bones but words will never hurt me? Nothing could be further from the truth. For more information on this topic, go to: http://r-word.org

Music to My Ears
by Tina Traster

There we were, on our winter break vacation, driving to our hotel after a day of skiing in the Canadian Laurentians.

"I miss my violin," Julia sighed, dreamily gazing out at the frozen tundra, not really talking to either my husband nor I. Just thinking out loud.

"Really?" I said, whipping my head around to the back seat.

"Yeah, I should have brought it with me," she lamented. "I miss it."

A smile spread across my face. Angels were singing. Julia's words were nothing less than music to my ears.

Julia is good at violin, and getting better all the time. Is she destined for Lincoln Center? I doubt it. That's not the point. The fact that she was missing her violin was not about future musical accomplishment. That she was "missing" something was what made this the screech-on-the-brakes moment. It's not like Julia to make a deep attachment or commitment to something, to anything. She's innately intelligent so she pretty much gallops by at whatever she does or has to do.

But showing passion, well, this was new.

Julia uttered this comment on practically her 10th "Gotcha" anniversary, the day we "got her" from Russia. She was eight months old when we adopted her from Siberia a decade ago. Though she was young, Julia had trouble attaching to anyone — or anything — from the moment we brought her home. She never laid claim to a teddy bear or a favorite blanket or toy. She didn't attach to me or my husband, or to other caretakers. She never made a good friend. She was like a drifter, taking what she needed, passing through.

When we found a name for this — Reactive Attachment Disorder — we made it our life's work to pull Julia out of her dark tunnel. It took years; it's never the kind of thing that's completely healed. By the time she was four, we fully understood the syndrome, which is caused by early separation from a birth mother. Babies who don't get the nurture and love they deserve subconsciously learn it's better not to attach to anyone or anything because everything in life, especially love, is ephemeral. A harsh lesson for an infant.

Still, that is what they learn, and these children have a crafty way of keeping their distance, and making sure nothing matters too much. It reminds you of someone who's been burned by divorce and decides to close their heart.

At ten, Julia is fully attached to my husband and me. We are a solid forever family, the three of us. But our daughter is still reticent about investing her passion elsewhere. There are no posters of Justin Bieber in her room. No friend from school she calls her BFF. No one thing that really, really matters.

Except maybe her violin?

She took it up in fourth grade. She didn't show any particular talent or interest in the instrument. She never practiced at home, but she coasted in the year-end performance. I thought that was the end of that. Then she went to a sleep-away camp for the performing arts. I had been expecting her to be in one of the theatrical shows but when we got there on visiting day she played violin in a strings concert.

When she returned home, I hired a private music teacher, Karen. Magical things happened. Julia loves Karen. Karen adores Julia. Julia is getting real good on the violin. She practices every day for 30 minutes. She shows commitment. Passion, even. Music has led her to some part of herself that has cracked open resistance to taking chances and to loving something.

A week ago, I told Julia we were going to her grandmother's for Passover. Grandma was expecting 15 people.

"Can I bring my violin and play it for everyone?" she asked.

"Please do," I replied with a smile.

THE MEN

"Honey, you gave me some read good advice once, so let me give you some of my own. It's real easy to forget what's important, so don't."

Jack Butler

from the movie, *Mr. Mom*

Should We Take the Only Thing They Have Left?

by John Simmons

Perhaps we should. My wife and I decided that it was the right thing to change our children's names as we adopted them. This happened across the board, from Jack, who was only a month old when he joined our family, clear up to Emily who was fifteen.

That really upsets some people. My kids? Not so much. Recently a mom-blogger voiced her disagreement, and so I decided to find out what my adopted children really thought. We had never talked about it before.

Whether or not I understand how it feels to have my name changed, my children do. (My eighteen-year-old with Down syndrome could have been asked the question many times and would have provided contradictory answers, so I'll leave him out of this particular story.) The children I questioned range in ages from twenty-two, down to nine. Four of the five said they preferred getting a new name. The youngest, my nine-year-old son, said, "I wish I still had my Russian name, but it's okay."

It is interesting that the one who wishes his name hadn't been changed is the only one who doesn't have any memories of where he came from. He has also not reached the point where he is ready to hear about his past. (His psychologist told us that when he was ready, he would ask questions and that then we should answer those questions honestly, and wait until he was ready for more.)

Our children who prefer their new names don't wonder if they were kidnapped and sold on the black market. They don't think that a loving birth-mother and birth-father gave them away to wealthy Americans. They don't wonder if a birth-mother was pressured into giving them away, against her will, because of what society or religion might have thought. My four daughters know where they came from and it was a life of horrific abuse. It took an incredible amount of work on our part to get them to even tolerate our speaking well of Russia. To them, Russia was nothing more than an abusive home, and then an orphanage. *Amérika* was Utopia. They wanted to forget where they had come from, and with the exception of a few friends, everything about that place. Perhaps that is why a name change was to their preference. I don't know. I can tell you, though; those circumstances were not part of our decision to change their names.

Amy and I had three sons biologically before we began adopting. That culminated in adding one more child by domestic adoption, and five more from Russia. Amy and I put a lot of thought into the names of our first three sons. Their names had meaning to us and some had family ties. When we adopted our other children, we wanted them to feel like they were just like other members of our family. We wanted them to feel like they were just like other members of our community. I'll now admit; that was naïve thinking. Of course there are times when they feel different. Maybe the name changes reduced that. Maybe they didn't.

Each of our five children from Russia bear the names of ancestors of either Amy or me, who left their native lands and migrated to the United States. We have used the stories of those ancestors to show our children that they are not the only ones in our family who left native lands behind. We teach them that emigration is never easy, but that with hard work, it can be worth it. Our children know that our reasons for changing their names were based on love and wanting the best for them. Perhaps that is why Denney (maiden name of my mother, and surname to Charles Denney, the first from that family to leave England) cuts me some slack.

I'm sure that my "on the job training" of being a dad will cause my children some difficulties. It has been like learning to drive during the Indianapolis 500. I have made plenty of mistakes and one thing is sure: I'll make plenty more. But I hope my children, whether added to our family biologically or through adoption, always understand that I tried to do my best with the knowledge I had available to me. And I hope, most of all, they always know I love them.

How I Overcame My Fear of Being Mistaken for Grandpa

by Len Filppu

When my wife was pregnant with our first child, we joined another expectant couple for a snack after our prenatal class. They were a typical demographic of this class, young, bright-eyed and fresh, unwrinkled, unworn, and eager to learn what lay ahead in parenthood. Their youth and enthusiasm unnerved me because I was then 49 years-old and facing fatherhood for the first time. I ordered coffee and cherry pie a la mode.

Weeks earlier on the first night of our prenatal class, before I had even looked at the class instructor, I'd quickly checked out the 20 or so other couples in attendance and easily determined I was the oldest man there. So, despite the fact that my wife tells me I look 10 years younger than my age and I think of myself as an active and hip dude, I felt old, out of place, a trespasser on this chatter of children soon to give birth to children.

Somehow, innocently, the conversation turned to age. The couple announced they were in their 20s, working on some dot-com pipe dream, and how the future was bright with fortune and family. My then-37-year-old wife responded with a comment about the dampening of her ticking clock, and then everyone casually looked at me, naturally.

Now, in a normal course of light and polite conversation, I would pick up the thread and express my take on any situation. But I didn't feel normal that night. I was suddenly intensely self-conscious and embarrassed at being such a Methuselah. Wishing to avoid confronting the truth, I looked down into my pie for something to say. The slick red dye of the cherry pie filling looked garish and artificial in the diner's bright light... exactly how I felt.

My wife must have said something to start time moving again, but I don't remember. What I do recall, vividly, is the sinking feeling of being struck dumb and sabotaged by my own stinking thinking that I was too old for fatherhood. I was astonished by my sudden fear of letting others know my true age, and at how deeply this issue affected me. I realized, as though I just discovered a nail stuck in my car's tire, that if forward progress were to proceed, I needed to do something about it soon.

I didn't immediately share my feelings with Lucy or anyone else. I'm old school in that respect. At the first whiff of a problem, Lucy reflexively phones friends, family, confidants, and guiding influences to air and sort out her feelings. On the opposite end of the share-your-pain spectrum, I tend to work through my issues myself, mulling them over, exploring their importance, and figuring out ways to avoid and ignore them. Seeking the advice and support of others is only done as a last resort.

So, as the California sun shone bright the next day and I headed off to work managing a high technology communications agency, I instinctively followed my habitual path of problem solving by refocusing on the day-to-day realities of managing my staff, developing competitive strategies, and collecting invoices. I buried those niggling thoughts about being too old for fatherhood. I whistled past the graveyard. But this particular zombie refused to stay interred and continued to stalk and spook me.

What was it that really bothered me? Deep down inside I was tickled pink at the prospect of fatherhood, even so much later in life. I'd always wanted my own family, had enjoyed my role as uncle to nephews and niece, and all my close childhood friends were fathers and even grandfathers. I felt fairly competent and optimistic about handling the responsibilities of fatherhood as I understood them at the time. Sure, I was older than any other expectant dad I'd met, but my friends, family and in-laws were all supportive and congratulatory. I was healthy, had some money in the bank, and knew my wife would make a great mother.

So what was it? Why was I so bothered about what others might think of my age? Mulling it over revealed a variety of reasons. Sure, I was worried about feeling different, some kind of freak, of being ostracized and embarrassed. But these are petty concerns, more appropriate for teenagers than a 49- year-old man.

Slowly, the ugly truth slowly reared its hoary head: I did not want to be mistaken for the grandfather.

There it was, as pathetic as Grandpa Simpson drooling out his false teeth, snoozing in a misshapen Lazy-Boy while a hemorrhoid commercial blares too loud on the TV next to his walker. I did not want to be mistaken for Grandpa! Vanity invites insanity.

Then one day several years back, I experienced the psychological breakthrough that provided healing insight into my age issue. We invited two other couples and their children over for a cookout. During the course of the evening, all the kids followed my then three-year-old son's lead of stripping off his clothes and running wild and naked around the house and yard strumming a toy guitar.

The kids were squealing with joy, having a riot. I was

a bit concerned that some of our parent-guests might object to this permissive nudist romp, so I asked gently if everything was okay.

One of the young moms, barely 30 years old at the time, gave me a genuine, reassuring smile and said, "We just *love* coming to your house. It's like Woodstock!"

Wow. Her words warmed me like hot chocolate on the ski slope. This wonderful woman was not even alive when Woodstock surprised the world. Yet her reference reminded me that we parents, regardless of our external differences, share a common bond that deeply unites us.

We pull together as kindred spirits while roaming through this parenthood festival, sharing our celebrations and making the best of things, whether "the New York State Thruway is closed, man," or we're dancing in the sunlight or slogging through the rain and mud.

In just a few brief moments of reflection on her kind, inclusive words, I happily experienced the healing transformation of feeling fully accepted.

I realized that not one of my younger parent friends had ever discriminated against me because of my age. They'd always accepted me and treated me as an equal, just another new dad, fumbling around, back aching, trying to figure out how to do what's best for the children.

All my fears of being perceived as a dozing, drooling Grandpa Simpson had been unfounded, mere nagging phantoms inside my own crazy head. I'd tortured myself by comparing my insides to younger parents' externals. I had been my own worst enemy. I was the ageist!

What a revelation. This mature, former citizen of the Woodstock Nation (now finding refuge in the Colbert Nation) finally realized he was diminishing his own enjoyment of fatherhood by worrying about age. I now openly and honestly discuss the issue when occasions arise. Interesting conversations ensue. A 33-year-old father of two recently confided to me that he secretly felt *too young* for fatherhood.

I've come to understand that my fears about being outside the norm resulted from my own lack of acceptance of myself as a later blooming dad. It's an inside job. No one else seems to care. I decided to seize the daze and focus on being a doting, not doddering, dad.

I Do Not Own My Life Anymore
by Marc Parsont

I do not own my life anymore. I drive to soccer. I drive to karate. I drive to school. I drive to the doctor's office — frequently. I drive to fix the cars that drive the kids to soccer, karate, ballet, and yoga.

I drive to the grocery store. I drive to the grocery store. I drive to the grocery store again.

I am being driven insane.

I cook, but they don't eat what I cook. That includes my wife *and* my children. If I do cook what they like to eat, they aren't hungry. If they are hungry and I cook what they like to eat, there's (a) not enough, (b) too much, (c) it's too dry, (d) it's too moist, or e) all of the above.

They want to help cook, but won't eat what they cook, even though they like what they cooked and they did cook it. When they cook it, if they eat it, they may or may not finish what they started to eat.

They may or may not clean up what they did or rather what they didn't eat.

When they did eat, they should have used their knife and fork, but instead used their fingers. When they were caught eating with their fingers and told to use a knife and fork, they didn't want to eat anymore because it was (a) not enough, (b) too much, (c) too dry, (d) too moist, or (e) all of the above.

Someone has to do the dishes. Guess who? I do the dishes daily, sometimes hourly. Even if I'm not cooking,

I'm doing dishes. As a matter of fact, I seem to be washing more dishes than we actually have. Am I spontaneously combusting silverware, plastic tops that don't have plastic bottoms to fit on, and plate after plate of dried-on food? Where are all the damn plates coming from?

Then, there's all their clothing. The kids have more clothes than a Broadway production of *Cats*. They wear clothes once and sometimes not even that much. The kids change their clothes when they get wet or get a stain or get a wet stain. They change when they come home from school, play dates, and trips. They try on clothes and sometimes they don't try on clothes. Their grandmother buys them more clothes. They were on sale. They could go all month without duplicating their wardrobe.

That's why I do laundry, lots and lots of laundry. I do laundry in the morning, afternoon and in the evening. We go on vacation; I do laundry. We visit friends and family when we're traveling on vacation. I do laundry. We've been to friend's houses for lunch or dinner and wound up doing — laundry.

I buy laundry detergent in the economy Jeroboam size. I almost buy as much laundry detergent as I buy tissues. Tissues, or rather the lack of tissues, prove that black holes exist.

Otherwise, how can you explain how 20 boxes of tissues disappear in a matter of minutes? Even with the nanny and the dog, we only have six noses in the house. Where do the tissues go? Is there a tissue heaven? Is someone stealing our tissues?

Someone is stealing library books, too. I know this because neither of my children can find their library books to return to the library. The librarians are not amused. I am amused because the children ask me to find their books. I can't even find the top of my desk.

I could go on… but I have to drive the kids to Sunday School.

My Newest Career: Mr. Mom

by Doug Crawford

You might think it unusual that I read Parenting magazine, that I know women by their children's names, and that most women who speak with me are grandmothers — around my own age! However, what you don't know is that at age 53, I'm actually now the mom (The *Baby-Daddy*, too) of the household — not what I expected to be at my age, but one that clearly enhances and supports my family unit.

How does a middle-aged professional male go from Wall Street to Mr. Midlife Mom? Well, check your ego or id at the door, and embrace the precious gift you have been given. Then, love your wife, who, in my case put love for our son above her most important desire in life — that is, being the primary caretaker and a stay-at-home Mom. Her sacrifice for the betterment of our son set a high bar for me to live up to.

But let me share our story: Three years ago, after my wife and I received an email and phone call from our adoption agency and birth mom, I drove across the country while my wife flew to get our newborn son. By Christmas, we found ourselves brand new first-time parents. The adoption process and instant family is itself a wondrous story, but add to it my new role and you have the "new world order" — that is, stay-at-home dads. How we get there isn't as important as the fact that we are now here.

Please note that I do not take my new role or our role

118

reversals lightly, nor do I feel my son will be disadvantaged by having me be the daytime "go to" parent. If anything, he will come to learn how to do household chores and all the "fix it" chores at the same time. He will learn and play with Dad while we get things done, albeit a lot slower than it used to take. In fact, the time factor was and is the biggest challenge to being a Mr. Mom. Getting the "guy stuff" done while having an infant-turned-toddler attached is a feat Moms rarely do.

From an emotional perspective, being Mr. Mom has been a serious mindset change. No longer am I fulfilling my own destination through work or professional development. Now I have to trust my wife's abilities and focus on our son's development. It is, in one respect, a sense of loss, while at the same time a huge relief. The inability to spend time as I want is gone, as is the willingness to take on risk and stress. My independence of thought is now been replaced with how everything/anything will add to my son's development.

My wife has, in her role, taken on the stress of being the family's sole provider. That is, from a guy's perspective, a huge relief. For me, the real stress will be re-entering the workforce as a mid-age male who has been a stay-at-home dad. For now, being here in my new role is a creative process filled with laughter, love, and unique problem solving.

HERE ARE THE FACTS: According to the Profile America Facts for Features (CB12-FF.11 dated May 2, 2012) there are "**176,000** estimated number of stay-at-home dads in 2011. These married fathers with children younger than 15 have remained out of the labor force for at least one year, primarily so they can care for the family while their wives work outside the home. These fathers cared for upwards of 332,000 children. (Source: America's Families and Living Arrangements

<http://www.census.gov/population/www/socde mo/hh-fam.html> Table FG8)

By the same token, **17%** of preschoolers were regularly cared for by their father during their mother's working hours as of 2010. (Source: Who's Minding the Kids? Child Care Arrangements: Spring 2010

<http://www.census.gov/hhes/childcare/data/sip p/2010/tables.html>)

Questions

by Austin Wimberly

As a parent, I am used to my children asking questions. Thankfully, most of the ones they ask are easily answered. **What's for dessert?** *Usually ice cream.* **Can I stay up just a little longer?** *Usually no.* **What is the capital of Wyoming?** *Always Cheyenne.* But there are some questions that my children ask that require more thought. **Why is a negative times a negative a positive? How do I know I'm really me? Why are flowers pretty?** And then there are questions that have no answer. It is this last kind of question that has been with my family for a decade.

It was the day I met the two little boys who would be my sons that the question first came up. That very day, I was already anticipating that one day they would ask, "Why couldn't she keep us?" The orphanage director provided some clues, but the total information we had about her amounted to two sentences and a shrug. It just didn't make sense, and the more I thought about it, the less I understood.

It wasn't that I couldn't fathom the concept. I could. I had read **Oliver Twist** and **Les Miserables**. I had seen *Annie.* I was almost a year into the adoption process, so I was familiar enough with the concept of the word "orphan." I knew that parents are sometimes unable to care for their children, but attaching that concept to those sweet, adorable boys was proving impossible. And the question refused to budge. Why couldn't she keep them?

The opacity of the question wasn't the only thing

about it that bothered me. Any attempt at an answer focused laser-sharp on the fact that our family's very existence, in some part, depended on tragedy. In a perfect world, there would be no infertility, and my wife and I would have our own children. In that same Eden, mothers would be able to provide for their children. There would be no sickness, no poverty, no addictions. No orphanages.

But, as everyone finds out sooner or later, this isn't a perfect world. Tragedies happen. There's no getting around it, but tragedies need not defeat us. Tragedies need not leave hope desiccated and lifeless. Infertility and abandonment need not mean the impossibility of family. Love is adaptable. Given a chance, it can grow in the harshest environments, and where there is love, there is hope.

And so, we adapted and began our adoption journey — a journey of false starts and long waits, a journey that involved government bureaucracies, one of them formerly communist, a journey that stretched to the other side of the world and whose ending transformed our once empty spare room into a bedroom for two little boys. And we were happy. And they were happy. But the question remained, unasked for years but not unanticipated.

Only now, the question was somehow more foreboding because finding the answer meant finding out about her, and that knowledge would keep us from putting tight borders around our little family. That knowledge would open a gate that could never be closed. And I began to fear that knowledge, and for a time I avoided the question.

But as every adoptive family knows, the question won't be ignored for long. So after many years of pondering the great mystery of our family, I decided to do what others have done throughout history when faced with etiological loose ends. I created a myth. It took nearly seven years and, much like our adoption journey, contained many false starts and frustrations, but at the end of the process, my book, **Sobornost**, was finished and contained within its pages my very best attempt to answer that haunting question.

After researching post-communist Russia of the early 1990s and the challenges its women faced, after reflecting on what the orphanage told us, after scouring the internet and learning the stories of other women who had placed children for adoption, I could offer more than a shrug to my children. And, while I still couldn't provide concrete history, I could provide plausibility. And that was something, at least.

But beyond a plausible plot, my writing journey had brought certain truths about our adoption journey into stark relief. One such truth was that tragedy, even horrible tragedy, can become fertile soil from which good, even the greatest good, can sprout. Another truth was that, perhaps, the possibility of a human family isn't just some ideal but a real possibility that is always lurking just beneath the surface of all of our relationships. If what were once a group of strangers could become a family; if a series of tragedies could provide a fertile field for love to grow, what's to keep us from treating other strangers as family or seeing all the potential good present in any situation?

We need not ever feel alone because our next family member might be only a meeting away. We need not ever feel hopeless because there is no circumstance so great that love might not conquer it. And we need not have all the answers. Sometimes questions exist not to be answered but to be asked.

And what about my sons' birth mother? What of her tragedy? Her loss? Her loneliness? Do these grand discoveries extend to her? I hope they do. I believe that, somehow, they must. But these are other questions for which I have no answer.

Being Elegant
by Casey Kochmer

I am going to practice being elegant... I will start with my daughter, Mina, by focusing more on time to play and not being such a parent all the time. I will make this pinkie-promise with myself today, this morning... to not be *always* busy or in "parent" mode with her.

I am posting this here to help make my promise more real. It's simple to say something. Yet damn hard to follow through with your actions...(even with actions that should just be natural). It's all too easy for momentum, obligations, commitments, judgments, and so many other ideals or events to sweep one away from the actions we want to hold as our center.

Now this is a lesson for you the reader. Do you take time to play? Do you take time to explore your life...Or do you just make excuses and put off living till tomorrow?

A life built on excuses just means to grow old and die a life un-lived.

THE MYTHS AND EXPERTS

"The point of mythology or myth is to point to the horizon
and to point back to ourselves:
This is who we are; this is where we came from; and this is
where we're going..."
J. Michael Straczynski, American writer and producer

"Believe one who has proved it. Believe an expert."
Virgil (70 B.C.- 19 B.C.) Roman poet

Any recommendations or advice given is not intended to replace the advice of a qualified health professional. The information is intended to be educational and is provided with the understanding that each reader accepts full responsibility for his or her own health and well-being.

Reinventing Myself and
My Mothering After 40
by Kathy Caprino

As a 53-year-old mother of two — aged 16 and 19 — and a coach, entrepreneur, and author, my plate is over-the-top full, as is the case for thousands of women today. I work with women who are facing numerous crises in their lives. The top challenge for them? The utter inaccessibility of work-life balance, and the chronic feeling that they're letting down everything and everyone who matters to them.

To me, having a joyful and fulfilling life experience is about discovering exactly what matters most to you in life and honoring that. It's focusing on achieving your dreams and visions — as a parent (if you choose to be) and as a contributive member of society — but doing so *on your terms*, in ways that fulfill you.

I've found that midlife mothering is about that as well. It's about figuring out who you are — deeply and uniquely — and following your own code of ethics and values. Midlife mothering requires discovering what matters most to you, then having the courage, perseverance, and commitment to create exactly what you long for.

My family and my work are my world, and always have been. The biggest challenge throughout my entire life has been balancing what I want to do and be as a mother, with who I want to be as a highly contributive professional. These two identities had always clashed fiercely and painfully until I hit 40. Then things changed.

When I was 41, everything morphed. The crises I'd faced as a professional women all collided after a brutal layoff in the days following 9/11, and I realized it was time to reclaim my life and become a woman who could steer my own ship and craft my life as I wanted it. I knew if I didn't change, I'd be filled with pain and regret in later years.

But in order to be all I wanted to be as a parent and a professional, I had learn some harsh lessons — about myself, traditional gender expectations, my values and expectations, my relationship with power, money, and time, and more. I had to reconstruct a new identity that worked. I'd made *so many mistakes* throughout my professional life and my 10-year reinvention, that it wasn't easy.

At 41, I began to learn new lessons. I took each one on, made some big changes, and eventually found my way. Over 50, I feel finally so much more on track, more fulfilled, more in control and hopeful and courageous.

What's different now that I'm over 50? Here are the five key lessons I learned in midlife that have changed everything — about myself, my mothering, and my life:

Lesson #1: Traditional Thinking Doesn't Work for Me

I faced so much negative criticism over the years for being different from other women. About my working full-time when my kids were little, women harshly criticized, "I wouldn't want someone else raising MY children!" I've stepped out of that box of what women are traditionally "supposed" to do and be as moms, and I've done it my way. My kids are thriving, and I know now that we must follow our internal guidance (not the threatened, resentful utterings of others) to know what's right for us and our families.

Lesson #2: Enmeshment Isn't Good Parenting

I learned in my therapy training about the concept of "enmeshment" — being overly connected and engaged with your children (or others) in what they're thinking, feeling, and doing — is damaging. They don't know where you end and they begin. Being enmeshed stifles their independence and their development. I learned the hard way that I was enmeshed with my daughter, and had been with my own mother. So I worked diligently to build healthier boundaries, and provide the appropriate amount of connection and engagement so my children could gain the self-reliance, autonomy, and self-confidence they needed to thrive.

Lesson #3: Being "Superwoman" Means You're Super-Unhappy

In my 20 and 30s, I was driven to excel and achieve. I wanted money, power, responsibility, and felt my professional identity was the thing that gave me my self-esteem. Now that I'm out of that game, I find that my work lights me up from the heart and soul, in a different way than before. Now it's about helping people and about expansion and joy, not power. This service focus has softened me — I'm happier, more fulfilled, more self-sufficient, and I bring those qualities to my mothering and my family life, too.

Lesson #4: Everything Passes

Early on, when I was in the throes of a terribly challenging time — in my mothering or in my work life — I'd anxiously agonize and project into the future about all the possible terrible outcomes that could emerge. Now, I understand this immutable fact — what is present today fades and passes. Today's urgent dilemmas become tomorrow's challenges overcome, and these make you who you are. It truly is all good.

Lesson #5: My Best is Good Enough

I always wanted to be the best at everything. Now, I feel that doing my best is good enough. I'm better at going with my *own* flow, understanding that who I am may not be in sync with other women or men, but I don't resist that any longer. I am what I am, and I show up each day doing my best. As the beautiful little book *The Four Agreements* explains, "If you try too hard to do more than your best, you'll spend more energy than is needed, and in the end your best will not be enough." But if I do my best each moment, there is no way I can judge myself harshly.

At 53, my mothering is about beginning the launching process with my children, watching them mature and develop and letting them go. I know I had a bit of a hand in it, but I understand that they came into the world already equipped with so very much to guide them to the destiny they choose. It's a good feeling to acknowledge that while you're highly imperfect and mightily flawed as a mother and a human being, you did your best, and your best is good enough.

Soul Contracts...
Do Our Children Choose Us?
by Joanna Beth Young

The Angels are always adamant that we have a beautiful karmic bond with the Children we choose and that choose us, whether they be by birth, adoption, or fostering.

Those of us familiar with Soul Contracts won't find this too hard to understand when we realize that all of our relationships, but particularly those of intimacy and depth, are all predestined and chosen mainly in the spirit state before birth. In the last year, I've started to 'see' these bonds and soul seed paths behind people when they come for readings. They look remarkable — a cross between a star map and a string of pearls. Each strand showing us the agreements and 'destiny' points on our journey, with as much time and leeway as our free will wishes to join up, dot-to-dot!

When we adopt or foster a child, it is most likely a 'soul contract' which has been agreed before birth between you both as well as your partner. You may have been chosen by the child's soul as the perfect teacher, nurturer, or having the perfect gifts and ancestry for their particular life purpose. You may have also requested the bond during this life to help you on your journey to learn lessons, gain skills and also to experience another dynamic with a member of your 'soul group' on this side.

The Angels take our soul contracts very seriously and

help to oversee the synchronicities of this meeting and bonding, just as they would with a 'natural' birth. Therefore, your guardian angels and that of your adopted or fostered child communicate readily about what is 'actually' taking place between souls outside the "day to day."

Another most wonderful thing starts to happen when we adopt a child, which, when I first saw it, really surprised and touched me deeply. As adoption is a 'contract' we make of guardianship, once we take another being into our care and custodianship, the ancestral lines connect! So even though your adopted child may not be of your bloodline physically, the energetic DNA is directed to your child. This means they become of your bloodline energetically and are subject to all the boons and challenges of you and your partner's ancestral inheritance. This really seals the bond spiritually and it is this line that the child wants and agrees to connect to before birth.

Doesn't the child have a soul contract with their natural birth parents, also? Yes, of course they do, and part of that contract may actually BE to be separated, orphaned or adopted. There's a real gift in all of life's challenges that we may actually want to experience. Many people find soul contract knowledge very comforting and empowering when dealing with difficulties, tragedy, and injustices that they cannot understand. No one 'deserves' anything in life, and soul contracts certainly don't negate having healthy boundaries or making decisions that lead us to happier and healthier results! However, it does help us by assuring us that we do choose to have varied experiences so we can learn how to react and grow through them differently. We get a new choice every time we experience yet another setback, heartache, or loss as well as successes, victories, and gains.

Can we break soul contracts? Of course! Ultimately, we are spiritual beings having a human experience. I believe our challenge here on Earth is not becoming spiritual as we already are! It's being human that's the hard part! The Angels constantly remind us that we have free will, or else they would be able to intervene without us having to ask. We are here to take the credit for our own tapestry of existence. Children and parents can break their contract and move on at any time if they feel it truly isn't working out, just like any other relationship. In the case of fostering, it may also be that your 'contract' is to walk a short part of the path with this particular soul — to mentor, influence and protect them as they venture toward the next stage of life.

My own mother was fostered as a child and though it was only for a couple of years, they were extremely informative of her behaviour and 'shape' later on. The breaking of the contract in adoption situations is, in my experience, very rare. However, whether you have fostered or adopted, there is something very unique and profoundly special about choosing consciously your child/parent relationship during your Earth years together rather than before.

As a parent in this beautiful and unique relationship, you are cherished by the Angels as a true Earth Angel. Giving your unconditional love, guidance, support, parenting, and nurturing to another from conscious choice is really the highest life purpose you can have! You are amazing! Your Angels cherish and protect your child/parent bond and can be called upon to help you strengthen and flourish as a family.

The Delicate Balance of Therapeutic Parenting

by Julie Beem

The word I use to keep myself on the most optimal therapeutic parenting tract is: *Balance*. After reading, listening, talking to other parents, and attending countless workshops for the last 12+ years, I believe that at the crux of all therapeutic parenting theories is balance. Our kids need high nurture and high structure — both in mega-doses. And, I believe, that if you look at any of the "experts" offering therapeutic parenting advice, that high structure/high nurture is fundamental to their approach, but often called a variety of things. The problem is that we can never maintain a perfect balance of high structure with high nurture — but we can try every day to get closer.

I can only speak for myself, but I find myself always a little heavier on one of these sides. Sometimes, this is due to my own upbringing and background. Sometimes, it's due to feeling sorry for my daughter. And, sometimes, it's due to being tired and taking the easy way out. Therapeutic parenting is the most exhausting work any of us will do. But if your child is like mine, an emotional barometer, of sorts — you won't be able to get too far out of balance before things start to spiral out of control.

If I'm too structured and too much in control, to the point of becoming punitive, it trips my daughter's trauma triggers. I'm angry, and she's angry and scared. I then need to check myself on that one and decide what's important (my daughter or what I want her to do — my daughter, of course).

If I'm too nurturing, it can be just as harmful. Our children often get just as scared by a situation that is nurturing to the point that the structure becomes lax. They are often scared of their own angers and rages; they are often scared that we're not strong enough to take on their big negative emotions. (They feel internally out of control — so if we don't impose structure, they wonder if we are strong enough to keep our households from spinning into chaos.)

I'm coaching a mom right now who is living in the chaos of her son's out-of-control behaviors. She's scared of his behaviors (and you can bet he is as well). If she gives him parameters/limits, he rages. Yet she has to impose these limits because he'll then become verbally abusive, making impossible demands, and then rage. Either way, he rages. And, his behaviors continue to escalate because he craves the structure and is terrified of allowing the nurture.

Structure is necessary for our children to experience so they can then learn self-regulation, self-control. They can't learn this without first feeling safe (which requires the high nurturing). But, if the structure isn't held firmly, as the child moves on to a more toddler-level of emotional development, they cannot learn self-control and delayed gratification. My daughter exhibits much of this in her ODD behaviors.

Recently, she's not been feeling well (yesterday, we discovered a sinus infection). She's 14 years old, and I had hoped she was in better touch with her body to be able to tell me this herself. During this time, her general opposition increased. As a caring, loving mother, I attempted to nurture her while she was feeling sick, which worked — but only for the first few minutes. The end result? She was overly demanding and angry with me for tending to her needs — obviously fearful of her internal feeling of weakness when allowing me to nurture her.

My assessment — three possible things were going on in her brain — first, she knew she should be controlling her behaviors better (but felt sick and wasn't able to express that); second, she felt shame; and third, physical weakness elicits fear in her.

Shame is an interesting byproduct of our children's angers and behaviors. If we're punitive, we can contribute to the shame. But if we're not structured enough, we can contribute to it as well. Our children have a highly-tuned emotional barometer. They know if we're overdoing praise. They have an overly skewed negative view of themselves — so much so that too much positive talk about them makes them suspicious that the person giving them this praise is either: a) naïve, b) stupid (and therefore not safe), or c) giving praise with ulterior motives, and wants something in return.

Neither shame nor fear help attachment.

Knowing that my daughter needs a near-perfect balance of high structure/high nurture and knowing that I cannot (no one can, to my knowledge) maintain a PERFECT balance of these things, I listen for clues before choosing which side I'll err on.

Eating to Optimize Fertility and Good Health
by Cindy Bailey

Diet makes a difference in your fertility! I know from experience. At 40, after trying to conceive for over a year, I visited a popular reproductive endocrinologist who said I had a 2% chance of conceiving on my own. Devastated, I decided to do what I could to be in that 2%. I would not give up!

After much research, I put myself on a fertility friendly diet and four months later I conceived. I didn't need more evidence than that.

It makes sense, though. How we eat affects our general health, so of course it affects fertility as well. Just as a healthy diet can support your heart and fight against cancer, it can also have a huge impact on your reproductive health.

When eating for fertility, the goal is to increase the availability of nutrients that support your reproduction, as well as your overall health. You'll also want to eat to support your hormonal health — because those finely-tuned balance of hormones is so important to fertility and conception.

To do this, you're going to want to get rid of the "bad" foods, those which overly tax or stress your body, and keep or add in the "good" foods, those which provide wonderful nutrients and are good for the health.

I believe it's more critical to get rid of the "bad," so

let's look at what you should take out of your diet. The main foods (or substances) you'll want to eliminate include alcohol, caffeine, trans-fats, processed sugar, artificial sweeteners and overly processed foods (including all those bottled sodas and beverages!).

These foods have a negative impact on our fertility. Processed sugar, for example, negatively affects blood sugar and insulin levels, leading to hormonal imbalance. It also causes inflammation in the body and suppresses our immune system. Another example: Alcohol disrupts the absorption of nutrients, weakens your immune system and raises prolactin levels, which in turn inhibits ovulation. So you'll definitely want to eliminate these.

You'll also want to avoid, or eliminate, wheat and dairy, because not only are they especially hard for your body to digest, but they are also highly allergenic foods. While trying to conceive, you want to ease the energy used for digestion — the most labor-intensive function in the body — so there is more available to nourish and heal other systems in your body, such as your reproductive system.

As for the "good" foods, you'll want to eat an all-organic diet that includes plenty of vegetables (at least 5 servings a day!), lean protein, beans, good carbs, nuts and seeds, and healthy fats. Low-mercury seafood is also a great choice, in moderation, as are fresh, whole fruits instead of fruit juice, which contains too much concentrated amounts of sugar. Also, natural forms of sugar, such as raw, organic, or all-natural honey, maple syrup and brown rice syrup are OK in moderation.

If you eat meat, I emphasize eating it only in organic and lean forms. By eating meat that's organic you avoid added growth hormones that affect our own hormones negatively, and you avoid any antibiotics used on the animals. By eating meat lean, you avoid much of the dioxins — which are industrial chemicals ingested by animals regardless of organic farming practices that often settle into the fat of those animals.

Eating this way not only optimizes fertility and chances of conception, but is great for overall health too. Give yourself time to adjust to the diet, though, and don't skip visiting a reproductive endocrinologist (fertility doctor) to assess your particular needs.

In Praise of Older Mothers
by Rabbi Stephen Fuchs

The fifth of the seven traditional blessings recited at a Jewish wedding proclaims: "May the (*Akarah*) barren woman rejoice with happiness in the company of her children." The blessing is an acknowledgement and an affirmation of the recurring theme in the Hebrew Bible of the woman beyond normal child bearing age who has children. While the term *Akarah* means "barren woman," it is used exclusively — and in no fewer than seven cases — in the Hebrew Bible to refer to a woman who has children well beyond the normal child bearing age.

The first of these is Sarah, Abraham's wife and co-partner in the sacred Covenant upon which all of Jewish religious thought bases itself. In that Covenant, God promises Abraham and Sarah and their descendants: protection, children, permanence as a people, and the land of Israel. But those promises are conditional. To merit them we (as God said directly to Abraham) must: "Be a blessing in our lives" (Gn 12:2), "Walk in God's ways and be worthy" (Gn 17:1), and fill the world with *Tzedakah*, "righteousness" and *Mishpat*, "justice" (Gn 18: 19).

Sarah, of course, feels completely left out because she has no children. In despair, Abraham cries out to God: "What reward can you give me seeing that I shall die childless?" (Gn 15:2). Desperately Sarah invites Abraham to use humanity's first known fertility procedure — having a child with a surrogate — so that she can be a mother. She invites Abraham to cohabit with her handmaiden, Hagar, who bears Ishmael. Eventually —at the age of 90 — Sarah herself gives birth to Isaac.

Isaac in turn marries Rebecca who is an *Akarah* for 20 years until she conceives and bears twins, Esau and Jacob. Jacob marries four women, but really only loves one, Rachel. And Rachel is also an *Akarah* for many years before giving birth to Joseph. Three of Judaism's first four matriarchs, then, did not become mothers until middle age, and in Sarah's case, well beyond. Leah, who bore children shortly after her marriage, is the only exception.

Much later, Samuel, arguably the second most significant figure (behind Moses) in the Hebrew Bible is born to Hannah who is also an *Akarah*. The (unnamed) mother of Samson, the mighty warrior who delivers Israel from the Philistines, is also an *Akarah*. Finally, the great prophets Elijah and Elisha each invoke God's help to intervene and help two different women (both identified by the term *Akarah*) to give birth.

Hannah and Samson's mother share a vital common trait. They are steadfast, understanding and faithful, while the men around them (their respective husbands and Eli the High Priest) are clueless to the meanings of their divine interactions.

What modern lessons are we to glean from these disparate but related biblical accounts? The fact that a disproportionate number of the Bible's great figures are the offspring of an *Akarah* must be seen as a compliment to women who give birth during middle age or beyond. The many biblical *Akarot* (plural of *Akarah*) who give birth is testimony to the correlation between desire to have a child and the level of nurture and love that child will receive.

We all are all too aware of the many children born almost at random to young women who have neither the emotional maturity, nor the financial wherewithal, nor the family support to become mothers. Often their children are the results of careless "accidents."

The middle-aged woman who gives birth, by contrast, almost always does so with great intentionality and desire to become a parent. More often than not, the children of such women are eagerly desired, lovingly nurtured and raised in a home where finances are more than adequate to see to the child's needs.

The Bible in its praise of middle aged mothers goes even further. It sees their years of desire and longing as worthy of special reward. They not only give birth, but they "rejoice with happiness in the company of their children" who are destined to play an important role in the history of the Israelite people.

Later Moms:
Rocking the Cradle and the World
by Elizabeth Gregory

We tend to think of later motherhood in personal terms — often focusing on the story of each woman's journey to having kids at what is still sometimes considered an advanced age. But when all these personal choices are added together, they have enormous ripple effects, unraveling the old social fabric and moving us all toward a very different tomorrow.

Delay of kids, made possible by the advent of reliable birth control and our expanded life-spans, gives women in the 21st century a voice in shaping society that we've never had before in history — a voice that the world is only beginning now to hear from. And it creates a more equal family dynamic, shaping personal relationships in powerful, positive ways.

So no wonder increasing numbers of women choose to start their families later. Even in recessionary times, when birth rates overall have been falling, **births to women age 40 and over rose by 8.3% between 2007 and 2012,** adding their bit to the more than **80% rise in births in this age band since 1990**. Add in later moms in the 35-39 age band (also burgeoning in recent decades), and that's one in seven babies born to a later mom, and one in 12 first babies (up from one in 100 in 1970). Add to those the many later adoptive and step moms (for which there are no firm stats), and you've got a substantial portion of the population mothering later than their mothers did, and from a very different cultural access place.

The new human ability to control fertility offers women who want kids the chance to wait to start their families until they feel personally and professionally ready for them. For many, that means waiting until after they've finished their educations and are established at work. In our current family-unfriendly work world, delay works as a shadow benefits system, providing women with access to higher wages and flexibility, perks often not available to workers who start their families earlier.

This isn't always a conscious choice, and many other factors may also affect individual women's decisions (like waiting to find the right partner, or to accept that the right partner isn't on the horizon, or deciding that you do want a family when initially you thought otherwise, or moving on to adoption or egg donation after a history of infertility that may or may not have been age-related, or suddenly finding yourself a stepmom because you fell in love with a divorced dad, or just finally feeling ready to focus on family!).

But whatever your back-story, the economic, educational, and work-history benefits are there. And your children, your partner, and the world gain from your increased cultural and economic capital. You get a hearing now when you stand up for them.

Which doesn't mean delayed motherhood is right for everybody. Many women feel ready to start their families earlier. But a growing group of later moms has been and continues to be crucial to changing the options for all. Women who move up in the worlds of education, work and government have been changing the work world and the world of government policy from within, gradually improving the options available and bringing women's interests and concerns to the table. Not coincidentally, many of these ladies either have no kids or become moms late in their careers. What makes sense for them also benefits the rest of us.

Media stories often present later motherhood as a problem — set to the ticking of an infertility alarm clock. But that leaves out the big social and personal gains that women experience individually and as a group when they delay their families until they're ready — either by a few years, or by many.

The real story is the happy tale of how much positive control women do now have over an aspect of our lives that ran roughshod over us for millennia. While long delay does lead to infertility, many women address that through treatment or continued trying, or they find alternate routes to a happy family through adoption, egg donation, or fosterage. And once they get there, they're fully present in ways many of them would not have been earlier when they were focused on exploring the world and building their careers.

Rocking the cradle and the world at once, later moms are among the faces future generations will look back on with love.

The Sandwich Generation & Their Parents' Tarnished Golden Years

by Rosemary Lichtman, Ph.D. and Phyllis Goldberg, Ph.D.
(Her Mentor Center)

Parents of Baby Boomers look toward their sixties, seventies, and eighties as golden years, with the chance to enjoy the fruits of their labor. But what happens when those days become tarnished gold? What if nothing you or your parents do restores the shine you all expected? That's the challenge the Sandwich Generation faces when their parents are diagnosed with Alzheimer's, stroke, or senile dementia.

Today, dementia of some kind has affected 14% of Americans over the age of 71 and the incidence is rising. Caring for these seniors generally falls to their children, most often daughters. Studies indicate that more than one in three middle-aged adults now provide financial, practical or, emotional support to an elderly parent. Over 30 million American women take care of both parents and children. How these Sandwich Generation women, and their brothers in some cases, cope is of increasing concern.

If you are propelled into caring for a parent with a challenging issue, undoubtedly you will sacrifice a lot — time, sleep, emotional stability, money, energy, days at work, dreams of your own. Because of these extreme pressures, family caretakers report having some kind of chronic condition at more than twice the rate of non-caregivers. And research suggests that this additional stress can shorten your lifespan by up to 10 years.

Here are seven tips to help lighten your load as you care for to your infirm father or mother:

1. Be realistic. Give up your ideas of perfection and be sensible about the path ahead. You won't have the benefit you had imagined of involved and wise old parents in your life. Acknowledge that the dementia will steadily increase and they will become less and less responsive to you. Be respectful of your parents' dignity even as you transfer control over their circumstances from them to you.

2. Evaluate your options. Try to keep an open mind. There is not one correct solution for everyone in your situation. It is helpful to hear what others have done in similar circumstances. Listen to what they have to say and learn from their experiences. But remember that you are still the only one walking in your shoes.

3. Find resources. There are a lot of support services in your community available to you. Recognize that you can't, nor do you have to, do it all yourself. Contact local gerontologists, talk with hospital social workers, meet with health care aides, visit nursing homes, or join a caregiver support group.

4. Talk with your siblings. Be honest with your brothers and sisters about their responsibilities. Even if you've been in conflict when them in the past, resolve to begin ongoing conversations now. Stand up for yourself when asking for their help. And stay firm about finding a way to share the care-giving duties.

5. Take care of yourself. Explore effective options to decrease the burnout that is common. A strong support system gives you the opportunity to express your emotions and receive comfort. Set aside time for rest and relaxation, difficult as that may be to arrange. A sense of humor can get you through tough times, as you laugh through your tears.

6. Evaluate the past. Look at how the relationship with your family has affected your present way of life. This is especially important if your parent was abusive when you were growing up. Decide to let go of defining your behavior today as a response to the memories you hold of your childhood. Make up your mind to change your attitude in ways that will benefit you now.

7. Grow up. As you take on the complex chores of caregiver, you are the one ultimately making decisions about your own life as well as that of your parents. You'll mature as you reconnect with your family in a new way, possibly making dramatic changes. Trust yourself and take chances to achieve what you want, both professional and personally.

Just as in the aptly named children's game, tug-of-war, you, in the Sandwich Generation, may feel like you're in a battle zone — pulled simultaneously from both sides and stretched in the middle. It is a struggle to sense the breaking point, but it has to be done to protect you for the long haul. It's not easy to set limits on the connection with your aging parents, but try to place that relationship in the context of the rest of your life. Trust yourself as you design a plan that works for all of the family, yourself included.

Acupuncture for Infertility: Find Out Why it Works!

by Drew Nesbitt R.TCMP

Infertility Statistics

For many adults, starting a family should be the most exciting and fulfilling time in their lives. However, for around 25% of the population, conception can end up being a frustrating and stressful process which can ultimately lead to emotional and financial strain.

For couples to be considered infertile, they must try to conceive for at least one year without success. Despite the fact that our bodies were designed to create, there are many complications that can occur during the process of conception.

It is a surprise to many that the causes of infertility are fairly equally spread out between the sexes. That's right guys: you and your army of sperm are responsible for around 40% of infertility cases. Not enough sperm, oddly shaped sperm, slow sperm, and a few other abnormalities can all contribute to male factor infertility.

For women, it is around 50%, not a surprise to most, as the female reproductive system can be complicated, with many possible problems arising. Issues such as hormone imbalances, poor ovarian reserve and blocked fallopian tubes can all contribute to a couple's inability to conceive. It is also possible that both the male and female may be contributing to their infertility, which is why some health professionals encourage both partners to enroll in treatment. The remaining 10-20% are known as idiopathic cases — unknown causes...easily the most frustrating diagnosis for seemingly healthy couples.

Weighing Your Options

When couples decide that they are ready for help, they are often referred to a fertility specialist for tests to find out what may be going wrong (if anything). The results of these tests will help the fertility specialist decide what procedure will be best for the couple to try. Typical treatment options are IUI, IVF, ICSI, GIFT and ZIFT. Simply put, many of these therapies require females to take hormones in an attempt to regulate and enhance the process of ovulation and implantation. While these procedures can be successful, they are both a time and financial commitment which most couples cannot afford to make.

Because of these financial strains, more and more couples are turning to natural therapies to help them conceive. Some of these therapies can be used independently or in conjunction with IVF and other medical procedures. The most common of the natural therapies is the use of acupuncture and Traditional Chinese Medicine (TCM).

Acupuncture for Infertility: What Recent Research Tells Us

Everyone who comes into the acupuncture clinic wants to know one thing: "How does acupuncture work anyway?" If you are an acupuncturist, you'd better have an answer. There are two possible answers to this important question. One explanation is based on using the poetic framework of Traditional Chinese Medicine (TCM), which refers to "energy" and "meridians" and explains how we balance your "Qi." Although this explanation is beautiful in its own way, it can be tough for those who do not have a degree in Chinese medicine to understand. The second explanation uses modern scientific evidence from popular medical journals. Although less poetic in its explanation, clients seem to appreciate these more familiar terms.

The Acupuncture-Brain Connection

A number of very interesting changes occur in the body when an acupuncture point is stimulated... most notably, changes in the brain. Recent fMRI studies have confirmed this connection. When it comes to treating infertility with acupuncture, scientists have concluded that acupuncture stimulates endorphins which impact our gonadotropins (LH and FSH). These hormones influence and regulate the functioning of the testes and the ovaries. The better the reproductive organs function, the better the chance at conception. Moreover, this stimulation appears to influence blood flow to the uterus, creating favorable conditions for implantation. Basically, acupuncture appears to regulate our hormone production. Regulated hormones can mean regular menstruation, timely ovulation, ideal implantation and overall, an ideal environment for conception.

Stress may also play a role with fertility. Stress from work, financial stress, and personal problems all contribute to hormonal disturbances and therefore will have an effect on fertility. You may know someone who has gone through a stressful event and skipped her period. This is the body's way of saying "You seem busy... why don't we take the focus off of your menstrual period and focus on this other problem that you're having first." Acupuncture is well-known for its stress-reducing effects and acts as a beneficial "side-effect" for those going through the fertility treatment process.

Chinese Herbal Medicine for Fertility

Although most infertility research has focused on acupuncture, Chinese herbal medicine cannot be overlooked. When prescribed properly, Chinese herbal medicine can regulate the menstrual cycle to provide the perfect "soil" to plant the "seed." Many herbs are also very effective at increasing male fertility and can treat problems such as erectile dysfunction and low sperm count. Be sure to use caution when taking herbs; they are powerful medicine and should only be prescribed by practitioners with specific training in traditional Chinese herbal medicine.

Acupuncture and IVF: Better Together

Much of the recent acupuncture research has focused on Assisted Reproductive Technologies (ART) like IVF (In-Vitro Fertilization). A recent article published in the British Medical Journal (March 2008) concluded that "evidence suggests that acupuncture given with embryo transfer improves rates of pregnancy and live birth among women undergoing in vitro fertilisation (IVF)." These findings exemplify the power of "integrated medicine," the ultimate in East meets West.

Integrated Medicine: The Future of Fertility Success

Current fertility methods like IVF are truly miracles of modern science. Yet these techniques tend to neglect areas which play vital roles in our health which can affect our fertility. Areas such as emotional health, sleep, dietary choices, and stress management are often forgotten. Fortunately, many fertility specialists and medical doctors are starting to acknowledge the current research and are now promoting services such as acupuncture to couples who are interested in a more integrated approach to their health. If you are interested in how acupuncture can "enhance the soil to plant the seed," visit your local practitioner of TCM and experience the positive effects of acupuncture.

Don't Whisper, Don't Lie — It's Not a Secret Anymore

by Adam Pertman

My son was three years old and my daughter had lived on this Earth for just two months when I met Sheila Hansen. She's a tall, soft-spoken woman who laughs easily and exudes warmth when she speaks; she has the kind of comfortable self-confidence that immediately makes you think she'd make a loyal friend and a good mother. On that muggy July day, sitting in the conference room of a church in southern New Jersey, she told me a story that chilled me to the bone and forever altered the way I think about my adopted children, about birth parents, and about the country in which I grew up.

In 1961, Sheila was a twenty-one-year-old government clerk in Louisiana when she told her boyfriend she was pregnant. He responded by giving her the name of a doctor who performed abortions. The procedure wasn't legal at the time, but everyone knew you could get one if you wanted to. Sheila didn't want to. As frightened and confused and alone as she felt, the one thing she knew for sure was that she wanted to keep her baby.

Not until 8:45 p.m. on November 30, 1995, when her thirty-four-year-old son telephoned her after a determined search, did she learn she'd given life to a boy. "All I did after we hung up was cry," Sheila told me. Based on what she had endured, I expected she would feel only contempt for adoption, but she is wiser than that. While she knows the process is seldom as simple as people would like to believe, she thinks everyone can ultimately benefit if it's done right. Besides, Sheila likes the way her firstborn son turned out (she went on to marry and have another boy), respects his parents, and appreciates the loving home they gave him. "But I'll tell you this," she says, wiping away a tear but faintly smiling at her optimistic conclusion: "The system we had didn't work; thank God it seems to be changing."

After a long period of warning tremors, adoption is "changing" like a simmering volcano changes when it can no longer contain its explosive energy. It erupts. The hot lava flows from its core, permanently reshaping not only the mountain itself but also every inch of landscape it touches. The new earth becomes more fertile, richer in color. The sensation of watching the transformation, of being a part of it, is an awesome amalgam of anxiety and exhilaration. The metamorphosis itself is breathtaking. Before our eyes, in our homes and schools and media and workplaces, America is forever changing adoption even as adoption is forever changing America.

This is nothing less than a revolution. After decades of incremental improvements and tinkering at the margins, adoption is reshaping itself to the core. It is shedding its corrosive stigmas and rejecting its secretive past; states are revising their laws, and agencies are rewriting their rules, even as the Internet is rendering them obsolete, especially by making it simpler for adoptees and birth parents to find each other; single women, multiracial families, and gay men and lesbians are flowing into the parenting mainstream; middle-aged couples are bringing a rainbow of children from abroad into their predominantly white communities; and social-service agencies are making it far easier to find homes for hundreds of thousands of children whose short lives have been squandered in the foster-care system.

Every historic phenomenon begins with a specific group and then sweeps through the entire population. That's what is happening in America today, complete with the trepidation and triumph that accompany all cultural upheavals. The emerging new realities undeniably are replete with problems and paradoxes. They are raising new issues for families and creating new dilemmas for the country. But they also are more sensible, more humane, and more focused on children's well-being than the realities being left behind.

Americans can feel something happening around them, and even *to* them, but most haven't identified the revolution for what it is. They assume, as we all mistakenly do about so many aspects of life, that only the people directly involved in adoption are affected by it. Americans are too busy or distracted to consider why they haven't been aware of the adoptees, adoptive parents, and birth parents in their midst (and they certainly wouldn't talk about it if they were), yet suddenly they see us everywhere they turn.

Of course, we were always there. But our existence was carefully cloaked, just as the history of adoption itself has been written, and hidden, in the shadows. Sadly, for too many generations, this wonderful and vexing process diminished nearly everyone in its embrace, even as it served their needs or transformed their lives.

I remember the moment it dawned on me that we all might be in the midst of a phenomenon bigger than just a sociological blip caused by aging, infertile baby boomers seeking alternative ways of forming families. As West Coast bureau chief for the *Boston Globe*, I was covering the O. J. Simpson murder trial at the time. Dozens of us reporters sat shoulder to shoulder in a small pressroom on the twelfth floor of the Los Angeles courthouse. I was typing my daily story, on deadline, when the interruption came.

"This is awful," said Diana, a computer specialist and the only non-journalist in the room. She was standing right behind me, rustling a newspaper and pointing to a story in it. I turned around and asked what was wrong. Diana showed me the offending article. It was about the Baby Richard case, in which an Illinois man won custody of his biological son from the adoptive parents with whom the four-year-old boy had lived nearly all his life.

"Imagine how I feel," I replied. "I have an adopted son." (We hadn't adopted our daughter yet.)

"Really?" said the *Chicago Tribune* reporter sitting at my left elbow. "I've got two adopted kids."

The *Time* magazine correspondent to his left looked amazed. "I've got two adopted kids, too," he said.

Diana, wide-eyed with disbelief, whispered: "I'm adopted."

I was surrounded, and so are we all. Suddenly — or at least it feels sudden — adoption is being transformed from a quiet, lonely trip along America's back roads to a bustling journey on a coast-to-coast superhighway. The infrastructure has become so extensive that it has made all of us — not just adoptees, birth parents, and adoptive parents — into fellow travelers. We should do all we can to make this a smooth ride.

Losses and Gifts in Midlife

by Lewis Richmond

Since the 2012 publication of my book *Aging as a Spiritual Practice: A Contemplative Guide to Growing Older and Wiser*, I have been leading workshops and working with groups to explore how to negotiate the path of aging in today's complex and hyper-busy world. Among baby boomers one of the challenges is being caught in the middle between two other generations: children and aging parents. If the children span the ages from young school-age to adult, two generations expand to three!

Recent studies show that 35% of young adults in their 20s still living with parents — with more still relying on their parents for financial and emotional support. In addition, our parents' generation is living longer than any in history — into their 80s, 90s, and even beyond.

This state of affairs is new and unprecedented and there are no guidelines for how to negotiate it. Add to it the fact of a generation of baby boomer mothers who have in many cases pursued independent careers and are still working into their 50s and 60s (another new societal phenomenon) and we see that for midlife mothers this decade has become the triple witching hour for responsibility and stress — helping adult children, caring for aging parents, and pursuing their own busy lives.

The consequences of this multi-layered stress are predictable — exhaustion, frustration, resentment, and a sense of being trapped with no easy way out. I can describe this whole situation in one word — loss. When I teach about aging, one of my core themes is that aging is marked by loss. As we get older we lose many things — our youthful vitality and good health, our earlier hopes and dreams, our sense of openness and possibility, and as we move into our 50s and 60s, we start to lose friends and loved ones to illness, disability, and death.

So as these losses pile up they add to the feelings of exhaustion and stress. When I speak of loss in my workshops, peoples' faces become serious. They know what I say is true. I also point out that loss is not the whole story of aging. Aging can also bring gifts — aspects of our life that we have not lost, and positive new developments that aging has brought to us.

In the midst of the daily grind, it is natural to focus on the losses rather than the gifts. So I hand out paper and pencils and ask people to engage in an inquiry. "On the left," I say, "write down all the losses you have incurred as a consequence of growing older. Think of a loss as something you used to have that you do not have anymore." Examples of losses might be loss of free time, of physical attractiveness, of no longer being seen, of an open-ended future, of your children being young, of your parents taking care of you rather than the other way around.

Then I say, "On the right, list the gifts in your life right now." Examples might be adult children having a new appreciation of you, reconciliation with your previously estranged parents, financial security (if you have it), new friends or intimate relationships, and so on.

You can do this exercise yourself. Some of the items on your two lists may seem obvious, while others might be ones you haven't thought of until you picked up the pencil and started writing. Circle items on the two lists that are new or surprising. Which list is longer? Which list has more circles on it?

Once you have completed these lists, take some time to feel what you have done and consider what you have learned. People often discover hidden losses that they hadn't previously thought of as losses, and discern gifts previously hidden. Our unconscious mind participates when we make these lists, and the inquiry is partly a way for our deeper mind to convey its wisdom to our surface mind.

As a final step, review the list of gifts and apply a feeling of gratitude to each one of them. Gratitude is one of aging's hidden gifts. I like to say that gratitude is an inch deep and a mile wide. In other words, in the midst of activity and work, gratitude is always there, though it may be beneath the surface. Whenever we receive a gift our natural response is to say thank you, so do that now. "Thank you" will not erase the sting of life's difficulties, but it will ease it, and that, itself, is a cause for thanks.

Why Have Kids?
by Susan Newman, Ph.D.

Get ready to have your fantasies, beliefs, and perhaps your reality of motherhood challenged. Someone had to do it and Jessica Valenti, author of *Why Have Kids? A New Mom Explores the Truth about Parenting and Happiness* has taken on society's glorification of parenthood.

Valenti posits — and I have to agree with her: The assumption that being a parent (and a mother in particular) is as ingrained in our thinking as is how women are expected to care for their bodies in terms of parenthood long before they consider pregnancy or become pregnant. Valenti peels back the glamour most of us anticipate when we become parents to reveal the hard truths: Being a mother is not universally what it is advertised to be.

Why Have Kids?

Valenti explained *Why Have Kids?* to Rutgers University's *Focus Magazine*: "It's a cultural critique of the way parenthood is idealized and not supported in any way and how that affects people and their happiness. You're taught that you're just going to have children and it will make you happy and fulfilled."

In regard to much of the thinking that is perpetuated on parents and would-be parents who are in pursuit of being the "perfect" parents, for example, she asks: Why are we shaming women who don't breast-feed? Is breast scientifically best?

Valenti explores the imperative of giving up our lives to devote them solely to our children. One of her many examples of parental choice was new to me. "Elimination communication" (EC) or the no-diaper method of toilet training was new to me. Ardent followers of "EC" may balk, but infant demands are tough enough without watching your new baby's face to see when he or she needs to be held over a toilet bowl or straddled between your legs to urinate. "EC" demands a mother's fulltime presence. I wonder how a woman who is tethered to her baby 24/7 in this way can possibly think motherhood is fun? I realize there are women who do and I admire them. But for women who have to work or have other children to care for, "EC" seems daunting.

That extreme example aside, if you don't follow expected norms be they co-sleeping, breast-feeding, or "EC" for instance, does that make you a lesser parent? As Valenti suggests, "American parents need to support one another — especially those of us who don't fit into the 'good' or 'perfect' mother model." Even if your birthing experience was wonderful, soon the guilt about not being the "perfect" mother and exhaustion set in. The worry about parenting "right" and the second-guessing of friends and family (and self) leave many women feeling anxious, distressed, depressed, and fearful. Unsure and unhappy. For working women, the path to parental joy is even harder. The "Maternal Wall" raises glaring barriers and parenting obstacles for working mothers.

A Dose of Reality

Why Have Kids? is brutally honest in presenting what many women think, but fear saying out loud. To get motherhood "right," it seems we have to buy into the current thinking that it is pure bliss. Jessica takes issue with the need to "measure up" in ways that don't allow for a woman's individual physical, emotional, or practical being.

Jessica, herself a mother of a young child, had a difficult and frightening delivery experience — which I suspect was the impetus for her book. Nonetheless, she exposes the truth about parenting and happiness today. It isn't so much a feminist view as a reality check that offers sound ideas and, if followed, just might add more joy and happiness to parents right now and in the future.

Do Children Really Make You Happy?

Yes and no. Valenti points out that "Nearly every study done in the last ten years on parental happiness shows a marked decline in life satisfaction of those with kids." And that applies to both working and stay-at-home mothers. Valenti found, "If you are a working mom who has unrealistic expectations about your ability to balance work and family responsibilities, your chances for unhappiness and depression also go up."

Perhaps we all need to lower our expectations for motherhood and being the "perfect" parent until such time as social and political policies catch up to modern day parenting and women support each other without judgment. In "The Truth about Parenthood," a piece for the Huffington Post, Aidan Donnelley Rowley, the mother of three, tells an imaginary pregnant, soon-to-be first time mom what to expect and how hard being a parent is in finite detail. The friend concludes, *"Maybe this sounds kind of crazy, but I am looking forward to the struggle."*

Valenti argues that beyond the struggle, "The pursuit of perfection and the resultant guilt are sucking the joy out of motherhood." Her candor, as she told Carrie Stetler, the journalist who wrote the Rutgers *Focus* story, "resulted in a lot of hate mail." It is quite likely that her book, **Why Have Kids?**, and my agreement with the imperfections she boldly underscores will, too.

Some Myths and Realities of Open Adoption

by Deborah Siegel, Ph.D., LICSW

MYTH: When adoptive parents give their child's biological parents their home address, they set themselves up for unwanted intrusion.

REALITY: While in real life anything can happen, in the vast majority of open adoptions unwanted intrusions are not a problem. The first step in making an open adoption work is for the biological and adoptive parents to get high quality pre-adoption education and counseling, to help them clarify their respective hopes, expectations, fears and anxieties, and communicate these to each other honestly, clearly, respectfully, diplomatically, and nonjudgmentally as they develop an open adoption agreement that works for them. No one size fits all.

Part of an effective open adoption plan includes a clearly spelled out mechanism for re-negotiating the plan collaboratively as the participants' needs change over time. An agreement that makes sense during infancy may need to be re-negotiated once the child is old enough to express her or his own feelings about the openness in the adoption.

MYTH: The best reason to do an open adoption, as opposed to a closed one, is to get a baby faster.

REALITY: Open adoption is for the child. The child's needs come first, over the adults' preferences, as the child is the most vulnerable member of the extended family formed by adoption.

The most compelling reason for open adoption is that humans need access to information about themselves. An adopted person has the same right to access to his or her genetic, cultural, and ethnic heritage as anyone else. This information can be lifesaving now that we know how important genes are in cancer and other life threatening illnesses. The health information available at the time the adoption is finalized is incomplete, as more information inevitably evolves in the birth family as time passes.

In addition, we all need human connection and identity. When we are cut off from people who are emotionally important to us, we experience pain. As one adoptee put it, "The more love in my life, the richer I am." Even children who have never met their biological parents may pine for them, miss them, wonder about them, and experience a sense of loss that often goes unexpressed, and is unrecognized by those around them.

MYTH: Children raised in open adoptions are bound to be confused about who their "real" parents are. The birth parents in open adoption will have trouble letting go of the child. The adoptive parents won't feel free and entitled to parent the child.

REALITY: There is no research evidence to support these myths. In fact, there is a solid body of research showing that the opposites are true. The children of open adoption know who their parents are. They can understand adoption better because there are fewer secrets and cut offs. Most birth parents are comforted knowing that their child is okay. The adoptive parents who know their child's birth family feel empowered by their ability to answer their child's questions. One of the most important ingredients in helping children come to terms with their adoption is "communicative openness" in the adoptive family, that is, the family's ability to discuss adoption issues freely and openly, with empathy, nonjudgmental compassion, and full disclosure of facts.

MYTH: Expectant biological parents who are thinking about making an open adoption plan for their unborn baby choose open adoption to meet their own needs, not the child's.

REALITY: Many people hold brutally negative views of birth parents. We say things such as, "I could never give up my own flesh and blood" and "the birth parents didn't want this child." Yet the vast majority of birth parents terminate their parental rights reluctantly, with great pain and ambivalence. Those who terminate voluntarily do so because they deeply believe that they are unable to parent this child at this time in their lives adequately, and that their child deserves what they are unable to provide.

Birth parents may recognize that their child will have questions that only the birth parent can answer; they recognize that in giving birth they take on certain responsibilities that no one else can fulfill. One of those responsibilities is to be available to their child, if the child needs that at times, and at other times to keep a distance, if that's what the child needs at the moment.

Given their great loss and their wish for their child to be safe and well cared for, the vast majority of birth parents do not want to hurt the adoptive family.

MYTH: Most adoptive parents end up regretting having openness in their adoption, wishing for less rather than more contact with their child's birth family.

REALITY: Actually, according to research, some adoptive parents may enter open adoption with trepidation, somewhat anxious about the unknown that lies ahead. As time passes, however, most adoptive parents' anxieties are allayed by the reality of their experience. Over time, nothing untoward happens. They develop warm, respectful relationships with the birth parents; adoptive parents come to see that the birth parents give them their blessing to parent the child and want only the best for the adoptive family. Adoptive parents who may have entered open adoption timidly come to value openness and endorse it.

Rather than wishing for less contact, when adoptive parents are uncomfortable with the contact they have, usually it's because they wish for more, rather than less contact with the child's birth family. This tends to be true as well for the child who is adopted. Adoptees in open adoption who are discontent with the amount of contact they have with their biological families tend to wish for more, not less, contact. However, most adoptees in open adoption are content with the amount and type of contact they have. The more voice and choice the adoptive parent, adoptee, and birth parent have in deciding the nature of contact, the more satisfied they feel.

MYTH: An open adoption may work out all right when the child is too young to know what's going on, but just wait until adolescence when the child is old enough to play one parent off against the other.

REALITY: When the adoptive and birth parents communicate honestly and respectfully with one another, they are able to navigate disagreements and discomforts in their relationships with each other. This means that the

The *ZEN* of Midlife Mothering

child is less able to "divide and conquer." In one example that arose in my research, a fifteen year old boy said to his birthmother, "I can't stand my mom. She won't let me do anything. I want to come live with you!" His birthmother responded, "Every teen feels that way some times. Your mom is your mom. Like it or not, she's the one you have to live with." Then his birthmother shared the incident with the boy's adoptive parents, who thanked her for her support.

171

My Debunking of Myths Regarding Teens in Foster Care

by Joanie Siegel

MYTH: Children do not want parents who are culturally or racially different.

FACT: A child/teen wants a parent, a person they can lean on and who will be there, no matter what. As long as their race and ethnicity is respected and honored, most children don't care who their parents are.

MYTH: All teens in foster care are there because they are juvenile delinquents.

FACT: Most teens in foster care are there for the same reason younger children are in foster care: because someone abused or neglected them.

MYTH: By the time a child is a teen, their personality is set and you cannot have any influence on them.

FACT: Recent research into the brain shows that a person's brain does not stop growing and changing until a person is in their 20s. In fact, more credence is now being given to environmental factors.

http://www.pbs.org/wgbh/pages/frontline/shows/teenbrain/work/adolescent.html

MYTH: Teens in foster care do not want parents.

FACT: No teenager thinks they need a parent, but they all want one. Most of us had to suffer through our parents' stupidity during our adolescence. Mark Twain said, "When I was a boy of 14, my father was so ignorant I could hardly stand to have the old man around. But when I got to be 21, I was astonished at how much the old man had learned in seven years." Deep down, all teens want is someone to accept them no matter what — even (or perhaps, especially) teens in foster care.

MYTH: Kids who leave foster care with no family are fine.

FACT: Youth who leave foster care without a permanent connection to a family (either through legal or moral adoption) are more likely to become homeless, be on public assistance, be incarcerated or die, than youth with a family. In fact, in New York City, the organization *You Gotta Believe!, The Older Child Adoption and Permanency Movement, Inc.*, which helps to find and support permanent parents for youth in foster care, categorizes itself as a "homelessness prevention program." In today's current climate, 56% of all children between 18 and 24 live with their parents. http://www.pewsocialtrends.org/2013/08/01/a-rising-share-of-young-adults-live-in-their-parents-home/ Youth who leave care without a stable family connection do not have access to this safety net.

MYTH: The foster care system has enough parents.

FACT: According to adoptuskids.org/meet-the-children there are approximately 104,000 children in care in the United States who need parents.

MYTH: The foster care system is too broken to fix it.

FACT: Hard working people try every day to improve the system. The more that dedicated parents push people to try harder, the better the system becomes.

MYTH: It is too expensive to adopt a teen from foster care.

FACT: For the most part, adoptions may be subsidized (that is, you might receive a monthly stipend until the child turns at least 18 and, in some cases, until they turn 21). Teens in foster care for one year after they turn 16 are eligible for college financial aid without taking a parent's income into account. Youth receive Medicaid while still in care or for the duration of the adoption subsidy. In addition, due to the Affordable Care Act, youth in foster care at 18 are categorically eligible to continue Medicaid until they are 26, if their state opted into that provision.

MYTH: Foster parents are only in it for the money.

FACT: Maybe some are, but most of us are not. We are there for the love of a child — because the system cannot replace what a parent can and must do to raise a healthy and productive person.

MYTH: It is not possible to love a teen through the foster system like you would your own child.

FACT: Yes it is. All you have to do is be willing to open your heart.

The Myths and Realities of Surrogacy

by Karen Synesiou & Fay Johnson

MYTH: You have to be a couple to be able to have a child through surrogacy.

REALITY: We are more and more seeing single women wishing to be mothers coming to surrogacy. Please keep in mind that there still must be a medical necessity to ask another woman to take that risk for you. Many women can still *carry* a pregnancy even after their own eggs may no longer be viable. While eggs may no longer be viable after the very early 40's, you can still carry a pregnancy into your late 40's. The average age of women in the U.S. carrying donor egg pregnancies is 44! We are also seeing many more single men becoming a parent through surrogacy.

MYTH: Gay men cannot be parents.

REALITY: Gay couples are more and more becoming parents together through surrogacy. They are sometimes able to use the eggs of a sister or the sperm of their brothers. Or they can use donor eggs. Lesbians are also able to use the sperm of a brother and keep the genetic connection.

MYTH: Now that egg freezing is a reality, you don't need to worry about having children until you are ready.

REALITY: Although technology is advancing and this may be a solution, NEVER GIVE UP TAKING

CONTROL OF YOUR OWN REPRODUCTIVE DESTINY because you think you have lots of time. Have your FSH (Follicle stimulating hormone) tested. Freeze your eggs, but start to plan this when you are in your 20's or 30's rather than waiting until you are 43. The hardest news to give a woman is that her own eggs will no longer work because of her age. If only she had planned this when her eggs were still at their best.

MYTH: The surrogate mother will keep my baby.

REALITY: In the history of surrogacy in the USA there have been 65 cases documented of a couple not accepting their child. There have been 25 surrogate mothers that are recorded as having tried to change their mind over relinquishment. Surrogate mothers and their husbands are as much afraid of you not taking your child as you are afraid of them not giving it to you. There are reportedly over 20,000 documented surrogacy cases, less than 0.001% have resulted in disputes over relinquishment. A surrogate mother can another have child of her own; she does not want yours.

MYTH: The surrogate mother is doing this for the money.

REALITY: If a surrogate mother cannot articulate several reasons why she wants to help a couple, we do not accept her offer to help you. Most professionals in the field believe that the money is not sufficient to reward a surrogate mother for her efforts. She must be able to recognize the internal benefits, to herself and her family, of what she is considering. As the Internet allows more and more surrogate mothers to advertise their services, we believe money will become a more important consideration in this field.

Most surrogate mothers probably would not do this for free. Her family as well as she will be making many sacrifices to help you have your family. Most couples would not want the surrogate mother to go without compensation. Couples often feel relieved to offer her and her family compensation. The couple can make a difference to her family just as she is making a difference to their lives.

MYTH: Surrogate mothers are low-income women without anything going for them.

REALITY: Surrogate mothers in most professional programs are already mothers, most are married, most work outside the home. Their families are self-supportive (no welfare, etc.) Couples have the ability to choose their surrogate mother and you can simply refuse a surrogate mother that you feel is not financially stable or appropriate.

MYTH: How do I know my surrogate mother will not smoke, drink or take drugs?

REALITY: As a rule, surrogate mothers feel a *greater* sense of responsibility taking care of your baby than they did their own. They want nothing more than for you to have a healthy child. That is why they have offered to help you. In REALITY, some surrogate mother's husbands report that they get jealous or angry at this pregnancy because she takes such greater care of this pregnancy than she did their pregnancy. The key to successful surrogacy is TRUST. She has been pregnant before, you will have met her children and realize that she is a good mom and that the children are healthy.

MYTH: Relatives or friends make the best surrogate mothers.

REALITY: Surrogate arrangements are more complicated that you think they are. It depends very much on who she is. Does she acknowledge the benefits surrogacy will bring to her as a person? Is she healthy? Is she a mother? Does she have a good support system? Will you feel comfortable raising your child in the presence of the woman who gave birth to him or her? Can you all make the changes necessary to resume your relationship after the birth? What will the surrogate mother's (i.e. your sister's) role in the child's life be? In one reported case the sister never spoke to the intended parents (sister and brother-in-law) again after the birth. Do not make a baby with someone you don't *like*. You may love your sister, but do you actually like her? Agencies have to screen hundreds of surrogate mothers to select the few that we believe in. It is difficult to imagine that you could screen only one or two possibilities and find an ideal candidate.

MYTH: IVF surrogacy with an egg donor is better than AI surrogacy because the surrogate mother won't bond with the baby if it's not her egg.

REALITY: AI surrogate mothers are not more likely to bond with the baby than an IVF surrogate mother. AI surrogate mothers are carefully screened (as are all surrogate mothers in our program). They have chosen the AI program in part because they are capable of making the distinction between their egg and your baby. Some IVF surrogate mothers would not want to work with donor eggs because one of the reasons they chose the IVF program was to help a couple have their own genetic child.

There are no reported cases of an IVF/ED surrogate mother changing her mind about relinquishing the child.

MYTH: Will my husband run away with the surrogate mother?

REALITY: No! We have not encountered any sexual interest between a surrogate and the intended father. All parties work hard to develop a respectful, warm relationship. Surrogate mother's motivation is to help a *couple* become a family.

MYTH: Will I bond with my baby?

REALITY: Yes, yes, yes!! Always remember that your child would not exist but for the steps you took to create your child. Couples are involved with the conception and the resulting pregnancy.

MYTH: Surrogate mothers are ultra-kind and altruistic women.

REALITY: Surrogate mothers are indeed kind and altruistic. Surrogate mothers still need your attention and kindness throughout the pregnancy. Not every surrogate mother is sweet and non-complaining.

MYTH: Surrogacy is illegal in my state/country therefore I cannot pursue this avenue.

REALITY: Even if surrogacy is illegal in your state or country, you can participate in our program. We only work with surrogate mothers in those states where surrogacy is not prohibited. Since it is not illegal to do surrogacy in these states, you are not breaking any laws. We are not aware of any country or state that prohibits couples from ever bringing home their child conceived through surrogacy. If a state or country prohibits surrogacy, this is usually limited to surrogacy undertaken in that state or country.

MYTH: It is less expensive to do surrogacy on my own, without a professional program.

REALITY: Maybe. If all goes well, your choice of surrogate mothers works out, and no complications develop, such as insurance disputes, psychological issues, or high risk pregnancy, etc. Almost all surrogacy cases work. Very few cases have gone to court. However, the Internet is full of stories of breakdowns in relationships and hurt feelings. This is less likely to occur when a counselor and agency are involved to work through possible problematic issues. You are paying a premium for our experience, attention to detail, protocols and contacts. You can do it on your own or with a professional acting as a matching service. It is simply more complicated for you.

A final **REALITY** that is often overlooked is what happens if this match does not work out? If you found a surrogate mother on your own you may have lost considerable time, emotion, and money. Many couples do not have the stamina to begin by themselves again. If a particular match does not work out for a variety of possible reasons, most agencies will rematch you in one to two months. Most always have surrogate mothers in screening and if one match does not work out, that couple becomes a priority to the program.

Infertility Myths
by Alice Domar Ph.D.

MYTH: If you just relax, you will get pregnant.

TRUTH: If only it were that easy! The fact is, the vast majority of individuals who have infertility have a medical reason, not a stress-related one. Upwards of 90% of all infertility cases are caused by physical problems. In the female partner, the major causes of infertility are absent or irregular ovulation, blocked fallopian tubes, abnormalities in the uterus, and endometriosis (a chronic painful condition where tissue from the lining of the uterus migrates into the pelvis and attaches to the reproductive organs). The male partner can have issues with sperm production which can lead to too few sperm, sperm which can't swim correctly, and abnormally shaped sperm.

Where the stress/infertility connection may come in tends to be after one has been trying for a while, and the stress of not conceiving easily may then contribute to the problem. But there has never been a study which shows that simply relaxing increases pregnancy rates. Research does show that infertility patients who learn and practice a wide variety of stress reduction techniques can have higher pregnancy rates than patients who don't learn those techniques.

MYTH: You waited too long to have kids.

TRUTH: While it is true that fertility decreases with age, youth does not guarantee fertility. Many men and women in their 20's have infertility. And women in their early 40's can get pregnant and deliver healthy babies. However, if you know that you want to have children, the earlier you try, the less likely it is that you will have trouble.

MYTH: It's the woman's fault.

TRUTH: Sometimes the fertility diagnosis lies with the woman, but it is just as likely to be an issue with her male partner. In order for a man to be fertile, he needs to have enough sperm (count or concentration), they need to be able to swim properly (motility) and they need to have normal shapes (morphology). Other contributory causes can be erectile dysfunction or lack of libido.

MYTH: Something you did caused your infertility (too fit, too fat, ate the wrong food, had a STD...).

TRUTH: There are few lifestyle factors which permanently impact fertility. Smoking can be one of them, but many people have stopped smoking and been able to conceive within months. Obesity and being underweight are both associated with an increased risk of infertility, but losing or gaining weight can relatively quickly bring you back to the fertile zone. Eating unhealthy food can put you at risk for diseases such as heart disease and cancer, but switching to a more healthful diet — focusing on fruits and vegetables, whole grains, lean meats, and dairy products are associated not only with a lower risk of disease but may increase one's chance of ovulating normally. Once again, if you know that you want to have children, it is indeed a good idea to look at your health habits and if you have any which might hamper fertility, such as smoking, excess alcohol intake, being over or underweight, extremely vigorous exercise habits, or a big caffeine habit, adapting healthier habits can decrease your risk of experiencing infertility.

MYTH: Infertility isn't a disease.

TRUTH: Yes, it is. According to the dictionary, a disease is a "disordered or incorrectly functioning organ, part, structure, or system of the body." Infertility in either the male or female partner is in fact directly due to some malfunction in the body, whether it be hormonal or structural.

MYTH: Having a history of an eating disorder won't impact your fertility as long as you are now at a normal weight.

TRUTH: Actually, there is evidence that having had an eating disorder in the past might increase your risk of having fertility issues later on, even if you are eating normally. Thus, if you do have an eating disorder history, it is a good idea to check in with your ob/gyn sooner rather than later, and if you try for months and can't conceive, you need to see an infertility specialist. Most cases of infertility can be successfully treated but don't wait too long to be seen.

MYTH: Infertility treatment is horrible and expensive.

TRUTH: Actually, many cases of infertility can be treated with simple inexpensive medications or procedures. A minority of infertility patients express high levels of anxiety and/or depression and many are hopeful that treatment will quickly lead to a pregnancy. While it is true that the high tech treatments are expensive, many infertility patients have some insurance coverage, and if not, there are frequently payment options and plans available.

MYTH: Adoption leads to conception.

TRUTH: This is actually one of the most enduring myths ever. The fact is, a certain percentage of infertile couples who "give up" trying to conceive then proceed to do so naturally, whether or not they adopt. Adoption per se does not make one more fertile.

MYTH: Infertility medications cause cancer.

TRUTH: As far as we know, there is no known link between infertility medications and cancer. The medications have now been in use for more than 50 years. We do know that there can be an overlap, in that some of the things which cause infertility are associated with an increased risk of cancer, such as never being pregnant, or having polycystic ovarian syndrome. So it is likely to be the underlying cause of infertility, rather than the treatment, which is associated with cancer.

MYTH: My husband is going to leave me for a fertile woman.

TRUTH: This is one of the most common fears of women experiencing infertility, yet the divorce rate in infertile couples is actually lower than that of couples with children. We don't tend to marry someone for their eggs or sperm, and it is likely that your husband simply wants you to feel less miserable.

MYTH: I had a terrible fight with my mother-in-law

a couple of days after my embryo transfer and subsequently had a negative pregnancy test. The cycle failed because I was so stressed.

TRUTH: We actually don't know the relationship between stress and IVF outcome. Many studies have shown a relationship, but they tend to measure distress long before the IVF cycle started. There has been no adequate research on distress during the actual cycle. However, it is unlikely that one fight would have prevented a pregnancy from occurring. Generally, it is believed that most cycles fail because the embryos were not genetically normal.

MYTH: Certain foods cause infertility so elimination diets can increase fertility.

TRUTH: Actually, for most people, eating a wide variety of good foods gives you the best chance of conception. The exception to this is gluten, for people who have tested positive for celiac disease. However, unless a physician or registered dietician has told you to avoid certain foods or food groups, based upon specific medical testing, you should eat lots of lean meats, fruits and veggies, whole grain breads and cereals, good oils and nuts, and the occasional bowl of Ben and Jerry's.

8 Myths and Realities About Adoption, from *Adoptive Families* Magazine

FACTS:

• As of the 2000 Census, there were 1.5 million children under age 18 in America who joined their families through adoption. This figure represents 2% of all children in the U.S.

• In the U.S., there are 5 million people today who were adopted. More than 100,000 children are adopted each year.

• 65% of all Americans have a personal connection to adoption and view it favorably.

MYTH: There are very few babies being placed for adoption.

REALITY: About 25,000 U.S.-born infants are placed for adoption each year—many more than the annual total of international adoptions.

MYTH: Adoption is outrageously expensive, out of reach for most families.

REALITY: Adoption is often no more expensive than giving birth. Costs to adopt domestically average $25,000, before the roughly $13,000 Adoption Tax Credit and benefits that many employers offer.

MYTH: It takes years to complete an adoption.

REALITY: The average time span of adoption is one to two years. The majority of domestic and international adopters who respond to *Adoptive Families'* annual Cost & Timing of Adoption Surveys complete their adoptions in less than two years.

MYTH: Birthparents can show up at any time to reclaim their child.

REALITY: Once an adoption is finalized, the adoptive family is recognized as the child's family by law. Despite the publicity surrounding a few high-profile cases, post-adoption revocations are extremely rare.

MYTH: Birthparents are all troubled teens.

REALITY: Most birthparents today are older than 18, but lack the resources to provide and care for a child. It is generally with courage and love for their child that they terminate their parental rights.

MYTH: Adopted children are more likely to be troubled than birth children.

REALITY: Research shows that adoptees are as well-adjusted as their non-adopted peers. There is virtually no difference in psychological functioning between them.

MYTH: Open adoption causes problems for children.

REALITY: Adoptees are not confused by contact with their birthparents. They benefit from the increased understanding that their birthparents gave them life but their forever families take care of and nurture them.

MYTH: Parents can't love an adopted child as much as they would a biological child.

REALITY: Love and attachment are not the result of nor guaranteed by biology. The intensity of bonding and depth of emotion are the same, regardless of how the child joined the family.

CYMA SHAPIRO

The Creator/Writer

"The moment a child is born, the mother is also born. She never existed before. The woman existed, but the mother, never. A mother is something absolutely new."

Rajneesh

"Midlife is the time to let go of an over dominant ego and to contemplate the deeper significance of human existence."

C.G. Jung

Midlife Mothering:
Ain't All It's Cracked Up to Be?
by Cyma Shapiro

When you think of mothering, you might think of loving, picturesque scenes of mother and child(ren). You might imagine all-things good, safe, and nurturing. Add graying hair, eyeglasses, drying skin, and a host of maladies including hot flashes, insomnia, reduced height size and memory capacity, slowing biorhythms, and you now have (new) midlife mothering.

As the creator and writer of a number of midlife mother entities, including the first art gallery show dedicated to women choosing motherhood over 40, I've worked fervently to engage the public in discussions about this increasingly popular trend, and help support women in their quest to achieve motherhood at whatever age feels right for them. My work has included interviewing dozens of midlife mothers ranging from age 40 to 65. With all of this under my belt, I thought I was well-prepared for whatever might lie ahead in my own midlife mother-journey. I guess not.

So, listen up — I have a dirty little secret: I'm not certain that midlife mothering is all it's cracked up to be.

To be clear, I'm resoundingly happy about my life choices: at age 55, I now have 8- and 10-year old children and 28- and 30-year-old stepchildren. You do the math. I'm happy to be a role model; happy to be surrounded by kids, and happy to know that I will leave a legacy. Heck, I'm just happy to be a mother.

However, there's an ugly underpinning to it all. Having gone through menopause, I cope every day with unanticipated body changes and the most sobering recognition that I'm on the other side of the goal post. And I still have young children to deal with and everything else that comes with raising a family. (Imagine rocking your baby to sleep while you are having hot flashes. I want to be alive for their graduations, weddings, and the birth of their children. Will I be?)

I am a member of the "Sandwich Generation" and have absent and aging parents (a sadness since grandparents were the staple during our childhoods.). I am also at an age when illnesses are striking my contemporaries in large numbers. My husband and I are not planning for retirement anytime soon. In fact, we expect to continue working for **10 to 15** more years, since we'll have children going to college well into our "golden years."

Although many new books have been written about reinventing ourselves and taking "me" time, we do not have the luxury to think about this. As mothers over 40, 50, and 60, I think we darn near "reinvented" ourselves when we had, adopted, obtained, or fostered our children!

I remember the first interview I conducted with a well-known entertainer-turned-mother in her 40s. She was a pioneer of sorts who had long braved her new older motherhood journey isolated and alone with her iconoclastic life choices. Now, at 62, she was bitter — her marriage was failing apart; her children were struggling, and she was fed up with it all. "Pheromones," she kept repeating, "It was the pheromones," as if attributing her demise to the sheer act of procreating for the sake of children. I remembered leaving the interview thinking, "What have I done (with my own life)?" But the strength of the warm fall air and blue sky that day washed it all away. Until now.

I was never jealous of younger "soccer moms", believing we all make life choices. However, there is strength in numbers, in making life choices commensurate with a clear-cut biological reality that allows women "down time" as their children are leaving the nest. There is an internal rhythmical reason that women choose motherhood at a younger age. For most of them, they do not feel nor stand alone in their choices.

Choosing motherhood over 40, we have braved innumerable obstacles and made many sacrifices just to get here. Unlike our younger counterparts, older motherhood did not "just happen." For most of us, it was a conscious and very determined path that we've chosen and fought for following in the footsteps of women like Frieda Birnbaum, 65, who had twins at age 60, and Fay Johnson, 66, whose unsuccessful attempts at IVF led her to embrace surrogacy using her husband's sperm. Her youngest is now 18. Fay marvels at how only by living in today's world was she able to employ medical technologies capable of giving her her life's only dream: children and motherhood.

Please know that I'm not seeking pity — just some compassion and understanding. I, too, did not foresee these obstacles when aspiring to be a (midlife) mother.

So, the next time you see one of us and ask, "Is she the Grandma or the Mother?" the reality is that we may be both. And we are also living a new world order.

The Love and Wounds of Adopting, Not Birthing

by Cyma Shapiro

I'd swear that I birthed my kids. Swear to you. You see, I regularly use this language, "You are *so cute!* Who's your Mommy?" (Meaning, me.) "What do you mean, where did you get your ears from? They look like Daddy's." And, "Everyone says that we're alike, honey." Freely. I don't think anything of it. In fact, on nearly every one of my younger kids' birthdays, my husband asks me in passing, "What time were they born?" before catching himself foolishly. Recently, they've started turning away quickly when they hear this, cognizant of the fact that none of us know, nor will we ever know this answer.

But here's the truth: they are mine, and they aren't.

Putin's recent stance on closing the door to American parents choosing to adopt children from Russia has brought it all back in living color and revived long-buried wounds: the ridiculously unpleasant experience we had adopting there; the very first look at someone who you know doesn't look like you (except in our case, they both do, in a way), and who you hope will act like you (they do). Wrapping your head around the fact that the tiny person in front of you is about to become a part of your family, if you and they choose to move forward. This is the experience that you swear mimics birthing, because the wind is rushing through you and around you so violently that you know that fate and the gods conspired to do all this without your control. Just the way I imagined

194

childbirth to be. Is it like that?

In cases of conception, women have several months to prepare and plan. In our case, the (anticipated) phone call was it. One nighttime call and on the next plane. This is not a given. This is when the wind picks up, swirling so loudly that you simply can't hear much except the pounding of your heart. You believe that this is your one shot, your one opportunity to have what you desire. And in many cases, if it isn't right, or if you've lost your place, or if... or if... you lose your chance, entirely.

You see, these are some of the other wounds that I carry: that I could not carry a child to childbirth. And that my children, one of whom insisted for years that he remembered being in my tummy, and I do not share. But some days, I would swear to you that he did. I often feel it.

We do share the ultimate hand-over. We share the first glances and the first real hold, both with fear and excitement. (We, too, also checked for five toes, five fingers and all the body parts intact). And, we do share the knowing that we didn't know when this would all start and how it would end. In all cases, none of us could ever go back and turn back time. What was done, was done, for all of us.

We share so much — my children and me. A fierce, primal bond; a ridiculous amount of love; an unsaid, unspoken agreement that we will do everything we can to make it work, make it all stick and make it all right. And I have a (more than) rightful place — I serve as a teacher, helper, mother, and sort-of friend. I am the person who has loved them and done a truly serious amount of work in helping them attach and be attached. But did I really have to work this hard, just because I adopted?

In the end, as I feel in all phases of my life, my

children have their own soul path and soul lives. They surely did come here "through" me and they will surely leave this earth with my mark on their hearts and souls. But somewhere, someplace, there are a few others who have had a tiny part in all of that. I always chose to believe that these phantom biological parents loved their birth children so much that they relinquished them to us. It's all good... isn't it? In this dance of life, I know for sure that neither I nor they will ever really know.

Regarding Having/Getting/Adopting Children: When is Being Done, Done?

by Cyma Shapiro

In a recent Huffington Post column, I laid out a concise spreadsheet on the positives and negatives of (new) mid-life mothering. I was hoping to educate people and engender a little sympathy and understanding. However, it seems to me that the vast majority of Americans still think that despite breakthroughs in medical technologies, a breakdown of the traditional family unit and the shattering of myths about women in middle age, there should remain a cut-off age to saying "no" to birthing/adopting/having more children.

All of this caused me to wonder: When is being done, done? Is "done" the exact same for someone as capable of conceiving as someone who must, or who chooses to adopt or foster? Should age, in and of itself, determine this?

I decided to go to some sources for answers.

For some people, saying, "I've had enough" helps save the relationships in their lives, according to sex and relationship therapist Wendy Haggerty, 41. "I spoke those words 'enough is enough' after about six months of infertility treatments that were not successful," she said. "I believe that the final time, which was a success in terms of the conception of my twins, was the last time I would have tried. It was the impact on my relationship more than anything that made me feel this way. There is no way my marriage could have survived another failed attempt."

For others, the chance to "do it again" seems alluring. "I'm not entirely sure I am done," said 43-year-old one-time mother, Michelle Fitzpatrick. "I would foster or adopt if my daughter (age 9) was older and more able to cope with that. And I'd have another if the right person came along and my health held up. On one hand, I think I should give up on the idea, but on the other... I've got this friend who has shown me some wonderful stories about 'older' mothers. My mom was my age when she had her last... and he was the best one!"

Then there are those individuals who just "know." "For the longest time I thought I would never be done," said writer and therapist Valerie Gillies, 54. "It snuck up on me, and I sure am solidly planted there now."

According to Elizabeth Gregory, Professor of Women's Studies at the University of Houston, and author of *Ready: Why Women Are Embracing the New Later Motherhood*, although the issue is complex, a family can come to both a compromise and an agreement. "I'd say an important part of whether or not a person feels she has enough kids is the amount of attention she feels able to devote to the ones in the house already. No use in endlessly adding to the family if the additions mean less of the necessaries for all," said Gregory. "This has never struck me as particularly sad — you want to be able to provide the energy, money, as well as the time your kids need. In addition, if you're partnered, you take into consideration the desires of both members of the couple, which will sometimes mean compromise — which, of course, should come from both directions." She adds, "For my family, two is perfect!"

Seeking more responses, I found the following diverse comments on several parenting websites:

For some women, health is the determining factor:

"I waited until later in life to have children so when I was pregnant with my second I was 41 and sick as a dog. I was so miserable; there's no way I would ever do it again. Plus, I figured I was too old. So I just knew that was it."

"I thought we'd have three kids, but then I had a cancer scare that resulted in a hysterectomy. We are very happy with two healthy kids now."

"For us, the biggest factor in deciding to be done with two was my misery during pregnancy. I spent the entire nine months in a haze of nausea and gloom. It was nearly impossible to take care of my older daughter when I was pregnant with my second... For us, it came down to, quite simply, we need to take the best care we can of the children we have rather than try to have more and not give them all the care we have."

For others, it is an issue of finances:

"I think it is different for everyone. Some listen to their hearts, and some people look at their financial, and still others think of how they feel physically to have more children... to not just have them but to raise them as well."

"I am not done... I have three girls but I want just ONE more baby. But hubby was done two ago. I have been lucky to have my three. But just one more... It is tough to know who has the more valid reasons, the need to buy a new car, the ease of the kids getting older, the march of time, but there is always just one more..."

"My husband and I (45/48) wish we could adopt again, but it is finances, not our ages, holding us back. If the finances fell into place, we would definitely do it again!"

Sometimes, mental illness sets the bar:

"I am in the midst of making this decision myself. I suffer with a mental illness and although my heart thinks I want another baby, I'm not sure my head can handle it. It pains me to say that. But I might just have to choose my sanity instead of filling that strong desire."

Still others use biology as the litmus test:

"For me, I think I'll know when menopause hits."

"I have two and long for a third... my neighbour (now in her 60's), said that the feeling of wanting another doesn't go away until menopause!"

Some are called by God's plan:

"I am 52 years old and had thought my adoption days were done. My next to the last youngest started college in September. God had a different plan. We now have legal custody... of a beautiful 6-year-old girl... I don't argue with God."

Then there are those who just "know":

"I knew after the third one. After the second one, there was always that questioning lingering, but my family felt complete after the last one."

"I have one child and it just feels right. I have no desire for another one, even though when I first had my daughter I was certain we would start trying again when she was six months old... So count me as one of the "I just know" crowd. It's nothing to do with money or pregnancy or babies, I just don't want another kid."

"I just seemed to know. We had four and the idea of adoption came up and I remember thinking: "I can do that. There's room for more." So we did. Then adoption was successful, and now I have five, and I AM DONE."

"I hate to tell you this, but I just "knew." I couldn't imagine adding anyone else to our family and before we had our last child, the family felt just not quite complete. I really had only planned on having one child, but now I have three... LOL."

And, finally, there are those women who clearly see signs:

"When you look at pregnant women and think, 'Thank God that's not me!'"

"When I could look at someone else's baby and not think that I would like another one!"

"When the paralegal handed me the clipboard in front of the house, gave me a nasty smile, and said sign here for the divorce hearing."

"We just adopted our first child a year ago and I will be 42 in February. My mom had me when she was 45. I've always looked at that as my cut off!"

In the end, for many, the sadness of being done is often the hardest challenge to overcome:

"It is so hard letting go of a dream and I don't think the longing for children ever goes away. I think that as moms, in our hearts, we love the baby stage and the love and joy we have from children..."

"I suppose — if and when we decide that these baby girls of ours will really be our last — we'll need to reframe our sadness over those missing "firsts" with another baby into a focus on the firsts that happen every day with the ones we already have. I have trouble, though, getting my head and my heart out of the realm of the 'what if?'"

So, as the debate rages on about when is too old to have a baby, the concurrent debate about "when does a woman know she is done?" also continues. But perhaps, the best answer is the one that is left up to each individual woman.

"To be 'done' is 'done' for whatever your reason," says Susan Newman, Ph.D., social psychologist and author of *The Case of the Only Child: Your Essential Guide.* "You may be done for physical reasons including health or age, financial reasons, adoption law reasons, to honor your partner's wishes. The reason a woman says she is finished having or raising children is individual and personal." She adds, "We don't know what goes on in other people's lives. While it is human nature to see things from our own perspective, to judge others or to criticize their family choices is simply WRONG and frankly, narrow-minded."

What are your thoughts on all of this? Are you through adding children to your family? Is your decision age-related? Lastly, how did you know when you had enough, and were "done?"

The Power of One

by Cyma Shapiro

It's hard to explain my (utter) fascination with Valentine's Day. On the therapist's couch, this near-obsession has been explained away as a move to fill an unfilled heart, response to a love-less childhood, and a push to find my own heart — all true, but not a fully convincing an argument for those accustomed to my ongoing madness.

Each year, I ruminate about the next holiday... well... after the holiday ends. Like my daughter's obsession with her next birthday, I begin formulating how I'll spend the day, who I'll send cards to and who I'll call/see/meet to say "I love you" and express my thanks.

In the weeks leading up to it, I'll buy V-Day boxer shorts (once cotton, now solid silk) for my now fully-grown stepchildren; the largest Reese's chocolate heart I can find and heart pajamas for my husband; a heart necklace and/or bracelet for my young daughter and the proverbial stuffed animal with heart for my rapidly growing elementary school son (who, at this point, is finding this a bit unsettling).

On the blessed (nearly exalted) day, I'll eat more chocolate, drape myself in red, and send/receive many cards that convey love, gratitude, and appreciation. I'll also traditionally deliver chocolate-covered strawberries (an 8 a.m. individually-bagged pickup at Whole Foods that morning) to those people who have touched me in some way during the previous year — many of whom are on the periphery of my life.

This year, I'll do so for my daughter's (school) curriculum specialist, my postal carrier and one of my doctors. A few years ago, I did it for the very unsuspecting technician who had given me my ultrasound, our neighbor, and both our school secretary and a crossing guard. My personal ever-growing collection of hearts (of every shape, color, and size) will now grace our dining room table on our heart-covered placemats, next to the bouquet of Valentine's Day flowers. Our string of flowery red hearts will drape across our dining room window.

On my midlife mother website, I'll take the opportunity to use the entire month of February to focus on love. I'll post blogs about: how to love yourself, how to love others, how to love your children, how to help your children love others; how to be grateful and how to live in peace. I'll offer affirmations and gratitude tips... you get the gist.

Most years, although my efforts make me happy, I wonder whether my small Valentine's Day gestures make a difference in anyone else's life. But, when I think hard about all of this, I realize that it is exactly the baby steps of One that help create the power of the Whole. And, at this point in all our lives, all across the world, we all need peace, love, joy, acceptance, gratitude, forgiveness, and loving kindness very, very badly.

So, I'd like to propose a challenge to you: on this day (or leading up to this day), I'd ask that you breathe in and breathe out images of love, and focus on your heart and its needs (be they medical, spiritual, physical, or emotional). That you try very hard to smile, say "thank you" and "please" whenever and wherever you can. That you acknowledge: the soldiers overseas, people grappling with terminal and life-threatening illnesses, those experiencing poverty and loss of homes or jobs, and those who have experienced nature's wrath and/or personal tragedy. That you hug your children, husband, sisters, brothers, parents, and friends a little bit tighter, as often as possible. And maybe start your own Valentine's Day tradition, like handing out (freshly-made, no less!) chocolate-covered strawberries.

Here's my Valentine's Day promise — with an umbrella of love this big we can make at least one day, in a very long year, better.

M is for Midlife, Menopause and Mommyhood

(The first blog post for the art gallery show,
NURTURE: Stories of New Midlife Mothers, 9/7/10)

For many women, life works like this:

Grow Up

Get a job

Fall in Love

Get Married

Have Babies

Grow Older

Babies go to college and/or get a job

Retire

For many midlife mothers, it more often goes like this:

Grow Up

Get a Job

Look for Mr. or Ms. Right

Look for Mr. or Ms. Right

Look for Mr. or Ms. Right

Marry, or not

Try to have babies

Get lucky and have children naturally. Use in vitro, sperm donors, egg donors, adopt, foster, become a guardian, use a surrogate. Marry into a family already with children.

Enter perimenopause
Become menopausal while
Babies go through elementary school
Babies go to college and/or get a job
Remain working

It's important to see this in living color — to distinguish us from our younger "sisters" — from other more traditional families.

For many of us, this is our truth. It becomes a hard thing to reconcile given the sometime insurmountable emotional, physical, physiological, and spiritual toll it may take, and the very fundamental financial component of it all. Add aging parents, peri- and/or menopause, reexamination and reinvention, facets of aging, two (or three) prior families, and all of this becomes damn complicated.

It's hard to navigate these uncharted waters at this stage of our lives. We often have few role models to emulate, scant resources to utilize, and we sometimes can't find the support we need from family or friends. We often can't find it from other mothers, either.

As new older mothers, we're asked to reformulate the images that many of us grew up with, the idea of partnering and then having children, or creating a traditional family unit which often exists, in part, just for this purpose.

But what happens when it doesn't go as planned — when Mr. or Ms. Right never shows up? Or age precludes the commonly accepted practice of becoming pregnant before hitting menopause?

What if the gears finally fall into place after the body

is incapable of producing this blessed event? What if the gears never fall into place? What if a woman desperately wants children, but can't, and doesn't have the money to pursue motherhood in other ways? What if she chooses to adopt or foster, but has passed the acceptable age limit?

These are some of the topics we hope to address here. We hope to also discuss daily mothering, daily spirituality, daily living. This time, it's from another mothering perspective: ours. We are front and center now, and remain right in the middle.

M is for midlife, menopause, mommyhood, and... maturity.

About the Contributors

Cindy Bailey is author of the Amazon top-selling book, *The Fertile Kitchen™ Cookbook: Simple Recipes for Optimizing Your Fertility* (www.fertilekitchen.com). In addition to giving talks on Eating for Fertility, she is a professional member of RESOLVE, the national infertility organization, and is on the Advisory Board for the International Academy of Baby Planner Professionals (IABPP). Her fertility story has been nationally televised on NBC and CBS. She is 48 years old and blessed with a seven-and-a-half-year-old son and two-year-old daughter. Both are the joys of her and her husband's lives, making their anguishing fertility journey worth it!

Julie Beem, 52, is the Executive Director of the Attachment & Trauma Network, Inc. (ATN) and a mother three ways (bio, step, adoptive). It was the adoption of her youngest daughter, now 17, that pushed her out of marketing consulting and into full-time support of other families who parent children from the background of abuse, neglect and trauma. Julie and the passionate board and volunteers at ATN serve over 1,000 families annually. www.attachtrauma.org

Kathy Caprino, M.A., 53, is a nationally-recognized women's career success and leadership coach, writer, trainer and speaker dedicated to the advancement of women in business. She is the author of *Breakdown, Breakthrough:The Professional Woman's Guide to Claiming a Life of Passion, Power and Purpose,* and Founder/President of Ellia Communications, Inc. -- a leading success coaching and leadership training firm for professional and entrepreneurial women. A former corporate marketing VP, trained marriage and family therapist, and seasoned coach, Kathy is a contributor to a host of entities including *Forbes, Huffington Post* and *AARP*. For more information, visit www.elliacommunications.com. Kathy's two children are now 16 and 19.

Douglas Crawford, 53, married for the first time at age 48. His previous careers included archeology and banking, capped by 25 years on the NASDAQ trading desks. He is the stepfather to three 30-somethings and three step-grandchildren. These days, he spends his time as a very happy Mr. Mom.

Alice D. Domar, Ph.D., is the Executive Director of the Domar Center for Mind/Body Health, Director of Mind/Body Services at Boston IVF, and an associate professor of obstetrics, gynecology and reproductive biology at Harvard Medical School She is also the author of numerous books, including *Conquering Infertility.* Alice can be found at http://www.domarcenter.com

Janice Eidus, 50-something, is a novelist, essayist, and short story writer. Twice a winner of the O. Henry Prize and a Pushcart Prize, as well as an Acker Prize, she's published the novels, *The War of the Rosens, The Last Jewish Virgin, Urban Bliss,* and *Faithful Rebecca.* Her story collections include *The Celibacy Club* and *Vito Loves Geraldine.* Her work appears in such magazines as *The New York Times, Arts & Letters, Lilith,* and *Jewish Currents,* as well as such anthologies as *The Oxford Book of Jewish Stories* and *Desire: Women Write About Wanting.* Janice has lived in The Virgin Islands and Mexico, and currently lives in New York City. She can be found at http://www. janiceeidus.com. Her daughter is now 11 years old.

Michelle Eisler, 43, became a mother at the age of 38 through the incredible, taxing, emotional, crazy, beautiful ride called Adoption. Having always worked with the public Michelle was surprised to find herself choosing to become a stay-at-home- mom. She spends her time doing the normal mom things, while trying to find the balance of also being a transracial and adoptive parent. A good day involves Michelle getting dressed, leaving the house with her now four year old, and getting home in time to make dinner. She lives in British Columbia, Canada. Michelle can be found at: http://mommamisha.wordpress.com.

Len Filppu, 62, is a writer/screenwriter who's worked as a communications executive in Silicon Valley, served as a press secretary to Jimmy Carter and on Capitol Hill, and helped produce a low budget horror movie. But the best thing he ever did was become a first-time father in midlife. Read his book, *PRIME TIME DADS: 45 Reasons to Embrace Midlife Fatherhood* (www.primetimedads.com), and follow him at *Huffington Post Parents* http://www.huffingtonpost.com/len-filppu/ and at Twitter *twitter.com/MidlifeDad*. Len and his wife have a 13 year-old son and a 10 year-old daughter.

Lisa G. Froman, 54, is the author of *Tao Flashes, A Woman's Way to Navigating the Midlife Journey with Integrity, Harmony and Grace.* A writer, poet and award-winning communications professional, she lives in Baton Rouge, Louisiana and is the mother of one son, Alexander. Visit her website and blog at http://www.taoflashes.wordpress.com.

Upon retiring as Sr. Rabbi of Congregation Beth Israel in June 2011, **Rabbi Stephen Fuchs** served as President of the World Union for Progressive Judaism until October 2012. In that role he visited 65 communities on five continents on behalf of Reform Jewish ideals and practices.

He currently serves as Interim rabbi of Congregation Beth Shalom in Milan, Italy. Before coming to West Hartford, Rabbi Fuchs served congregations in Nashville, TN, and Columbia, MD. He was ordained at Hebrew Union College in Cincinnati and earned a D. Min. degree in biblical interpretation from Vanderbilt University Divinity School.

Valerie Gillies, 55, is a Licensed Marriage and Family Therapist who works with young children who've had rough starts or scary experiences. She has been married to the same patient man for 32 years. They have five children ages 15, 23, 25, 28, and 29 – and more animals living with them than would be deemed sane. So she refuses to list them all.

Amy Wright Glenn, 40, earned her MA in Religion and Education from Teachers College, Columbia University. She taught in The Religion and Philosophy Department at The Lawrenceville School in New Jersey for over a decade. While at Lawrenceville, Amy was the recipient of the Dunbar Abston Jr. Chair for Teaching Excellence. She is a Kripalu Yoga teacher, a DONA certified birth doula, and a hospital chaplain. Her work has appeared in *International Doula*. She recently published her first book: ***Birth, Breath, and Death: Meditations on Motherhood, Chaplaincy, and Life as a Doula.*** Amy's son is 20 months old.

Elizabeth Gregory, 56, directs the Women's, Gender & Sexuality Studies Program at the University of Houston where she is a Professor of English. The author of ***Ready: Why Women Are Embracing the New Later Motherhood*** (Basic Books, 2012), she writes on later motherhood and the politics and economics of women's work on various sites and on her own blog www.domesticproduct.net. Elizabeth became a new mom at age 39 and 48.

Her Mentor Center - Rosemary Lichtman, Ph.D. & Phyllis Goldberg, Ph.D. are consultants in family dynamics. Whether you're coping with marital stress, acting out teens, aging parents, boomerang millennials or difficult in-laws, we have practical solutions. Log on to http://www.HerMentorCenter.com – sign up for a free ezine, "Stepping Stones," and download complimentary eBooks, *Reaching Your Goals* and *Taking Control of Stress.*

Barbara Herel, 49, chronicles her open adoption relationship in the Improv Mom blog on adoptive-familiescircle.com and is a contributing writer for *Adoptive Families* magazine. Barbara is also the producer and curator of the web series OpenAdoptionTruth.com. When not pondering her demise, interviewing, or writing, you can find Barbara dancing around the house to "My Sharona" with her daughter. She's also a fan of jog/walking or "jawking," and never misses a Wellness appointment. "Older Mom, Growing Older" was adapted from a previously published essay in *Adoptive Families* magazine (adoptivefamilies.com). Her daughter is now four years old. http://www.adoptivefamiliescircle.com/blogs/blog/us_adoption/

Randi Hoffman lives in Manhattan with her husband and 13-year-old daughter. She has written art and book reviews for the *Women's Review of Books, Tribes, New Mexico Magazine* and the *New York Blade*, among other publications. She studied memoir writing in Ariel Gore's Literary Kitchen. She is 54 years old.

Andrea Hopkins, 40, is a Toronto writer and mother of Claire, 5, and Anna, 3, whose journey to motherhood was informed and inspired by the international group Single Mothers by Choice.

Karen Hug-Nagy, 56, is the editor-in-chief of the blogsite "Welcome to Mommies in Orbit," created in November 2010. Karen is the mom of 13-year-old twins, Ben and Jen, and a pet-Mom to her two favorite canines, Cody & Nikki. Her favorite hobbies are freelance writing, photography and spending quality time with her family and pets. Prior to this, she worked in marketing for a satellite imaging company. However, it was at midlife that she became the lucky Mom of twins. What an experience it has been! http://www.mommies-in-orbit.com

Fay Johnson, 67, is a Case Manager for Center for Surrogacy and Parenting, Inc., dealing with couples all over the world to help navigate their surrogacy journey. She is the mother of Lily, 24, and Chase, 20. Fay is also a featured subject in *NURTURE: Stories of New Midlife Mothers,* the first and only art gallery show (traveling North America) dedicated to presenting women choosing motherhood over 40.

Suzanne Braun Levine, 72, is a writer, editor and nationally recognized authority on women, families, media and changing gender roles. She was the first editor of *Ms.* magazine (1972-1988), and the first woman editor of the prestigious *Columbia Journalism Review.* Her most recent published work is an eBook: *You Gotta Have Girlfriends: A Post-fifty Posse is Good for Your Health.* It continues the conversation with women in the new stage of life she celebrated in popular books, *How We Love Now, Fifty Is the New Fifty* and *Inventing the Rest of Our Lives.* She is a blogger for Huff/Post50, AARP.org and others. She is on the Board of Encore.org and a contributing editor at *More* magazine. http://www.suzannebraunlevine.com

Casey Kochmer is a Taoist Teacher located on the Big Island of Hawaii. He works with people around the world to turn mid life crisis into a process of positive transformation and a better life. Visit www.personaltao. com if you are looking for additional insights about mid life crisis. Casey had his daughter when he was 41.

As a 46-yr-old "Cougar woman" with a 3-year-old son and a 32-year-old husband, **Joely Johnson Mork's** life always seems to take a backseat to the rhythm, flow, and life stages of the other people living in her house. In her writing, she explores this topic with the dignity and respect her family deserves, while delivering the poignancy and humor we love to read. Joely has a master's degree in community health education and a certification in teaching yoga to people with cancer. Her son was born in 2010 after four miscarriages and a near divorce. A full-time freelance writer and editor, her work has appeared in *Prevention* magazine and many other print and online publications. In 2011, she relocated to Seattle with her family, and she is still trying to find herself at home in the Pacific Northwest.

Denise Naus, 40, is a wife and mother of three children – one by birth and two by adoption. She reads more self-help and parenting books than any one person should, but also enjoys mindless fiction and watching movies with her husband of 18 years. She home-educates her children and tries to navigate being an introvert, while having little people around her all day. She also blogs about life, family and her faith at www.pressing.com.

Drew Nesbitt, BA, R.TCMP, R.Ac. RHN is a Registered Traditional Chinese Medicine Practitioner, Acupuncturist, and Nutritional Consultant in Toronto, Ontario, with over 10 years experience specializing in natural fertility enhancement. Visit *www.drewnesbitt.ca* for more articles on natural fertility options for both men and women.

Social psychologist **Susan Newman, Ph.D.** specializes in issues impacting your children and family life. She blogs for *Psychology Today* magazine and is the author of 15 books including *The Case for the Only Child: Your Essential Guide* and *Under One Roof Again: All Grown Up and (Re)learning to Live Together Happily,* among others. Visit her at: http://www.susannewman phd.com

Wendy Sue Noah is 46 years young, and a single mom of five children ranging in age from 6 – 14 years. She is blessed to have a home office with several clients, working in the Social Media world. Her personal slogan is "Social Media with a Conscience." The flexibility of a home office allows her to be the supportive and loving mom she chooses to be, which includes retrieving her kids from the nurse's office when sick, attending her children's award ceremonies, or volunteering to speak at their school's "Career Day." As for cooking and cleaning, she gets by OK but prays for enough money for a nanny helper someday! Wendy can be found at: http://xeeme.com/wendy suenoah

Peg O'Neill, M.D., is a fifty year-old married mother of two boys, ages twelve and eight. She is a biologic mother, an adoptive mother, a practicing pediatrician and an Assistant Professor in the Department of Community Pediatrics at the University of Connecticut School of Medicine. Her blogs on parenting and child health have appeared in *Mothering in the Middle* and she has written numerous articles for the *Hartford Courant* on topics related to child welfare and advocacy. She is usually, though not always, successful in keeping her own children out of the emergency room.

Marc Parsont is a 53-year-old father of two children, one of each - ages 5 and 6, with Heidi, his wife of eight years. A massage therapist for nearly 20 years Marc just opened a new office in Alexandria, Virginia. Marc worked 11 years in the convention industry and prior to that, seven years in the hotel industry including the grand opening of Euro Disney, now Disneyland Paris. He loves to cook, watch bad television, read Sci-Fi and murder mysteries. Marc is not allowed to fix the plumbing in the house anymore. If his body holds out for another year, he also hopes to collect his black belt in Karate.

Adam Pertman is Executive Director of the Evan B. Donaldson Adoption Institute, the pre-eminent research, policy and education organization in its field. Pertman – a former Pulitzer-nominated journalist – is also the author of *Adoption Nation: How the Adoption Revolution is Transforming Our Families – and America,* which has been reviewed as "the most important book ever written on the subject." He also is the Associate Editor of the scholarly journal *Adoption Quarterly.* Adam appears regularly in the media and has been on programs including "Oprah," "The View," and "Today." He is a member of the Council on Contemporary Families, the Editorial Advisory Board of Adoptive Families magazine, the National Adoption Advisory Committee of the Child Welfare League of America, and the Advisory Board of Orphans International Worldwide. Reprinted from the book, *Adoption Nation,* with permission. Copyright © 2011 by Adam Pertman. www.adoptioninstitute.org

Liz Raptis Picco, 60, is a writer and blogger at www.stretchmarks.me, featuring **Stretch Marks,** her memoir about infertility, adoption, and writing. Her blog showcases her *guacamole with feta cheese* background (Mexican mother, Greek father, raised in a border town) and offers an edgy, no-holds-barred perspective. She and her husband live in Northern California with their two teenage sons. When she's not writing, she works as a health education consultant and translator. She's an alumni and active member of <u>Hedgebrook</u>, a writer's residency whose mission is *Women Authoring Change*.

Lewis Richmond is a Buddhist meditation teacher and the author of four books, including **Work as a Spiritual Practice** and the recent **Aging as a Spiritual Practice: A Contemplative Guide to Growing Older and Wiser.** He is the founder of The Vimala Sangha, a meditation group in Northern California (<u>http://www.VimalaSangha.org</u>). His personal website has information about his activities, teachings and writings. <u>http://www.LewisRichmond.com</u>

Kristi Rodstrom is a 50-something single mom living in the San Diego area. Her little big-man, Remington, 12 years old, is filled with laughter. And, although he doesn't speak, he still manages to get his message across. Her daughter, the enchanting Avianna, eight years old, navigates the world with keen observation, and makes up for Remington's lack of speech! These days, Kristi sticks to rollerblading, the gym, and hiking, although a well-worn pair of cowboy boots and too many stilettos also define her.

Monique Faison Ross, 48, was born in San Francisco and grew up as an only child in San Diego. She has lived in the Northeast for the last 15 years. Her four children range in age from 10 – 28. Some of her many passions include building a butterfly garden and doing home projects with her wife which help create a home oasis for their entire family. Among her must-do summer activities are going to her favorite Rhode Island Beach and swimming in the pool. She is currently writing a memoir and recently married her partner just last year.

Jane Samuel, 50, is married and the mother of three girls aged 19, 16, and 11. A former litigator, she currently works fulltime as a parent, writer and board member of Attachment Trauma Network, a nonprofit supporting parents of traumatized children with advocacy and education. Her work on travel, ex pat living, adoption, and parenting has appeared in the *Singapore American Newspaper, Adoption Today* and the adoption anthologies: *From Home to Homeland* (Yeong and Yeong, 2010) and *Our Own – Stories Celebrating Adoptive Families* (Touch Community Services, Singapore 2011). She blogs on parenting children and caring for elderly parents for several local and national online publications.

Cyma Shapiro, 56, is the writer and creator of *NURTURE: Stories of New Midlife Mothers,* the first and only art gallery show dedicated to presenting women choosing motherhood over 40 (now traveling North America), and the subsequent blogsite, **Mothering intheMiddle.com.**, which boasts a contributor list topping 100 writers and authors. Both endeavors are intended to dispel societal myths, help redefine middle age and women, provide role models to younger women, and offer this group a voice, face, and forum. Passionate about exposing the depth, breadth and talent of this diverse and burgeoning group, Cyma, a former journalist, now a writer, blogger, and businessperson, speaks and writes often about what she believes is the "newest chapter in the women's movement." In addition to being a mom to 8 and 11-year-old children and 28 and 30-year-old stepchildren, this anthology is her newest "baby!"

Ann Sheybani is a writer, coach, and speaker. She teaches women how to say no, create healthy boundaries so they can enjoy others without being sucked dry, speak their truth and still be loved, and uncover those dreams long thought dead. Fifty-year-old Sheybani has two children, aged 24 and 21, and four step-children, the youngest 20, the eldest 32. You can read more about her and her work at www.annsheybani.com

Deborah Siegel, Ph.D., LICSW, ACSW, DCSW is a Professor at the School of Social Work, Rhode Island College. Passionate about adoption issues, she is an adoption researcher, clinical social worker specializing in adoption issues, adoption agency consultant, and an adoption legislation activist. She has written and/or co-authored several books and is a speaker at adoption conferences. She and her husband adopted two infants domestically, in 1988 and 1993. For more information on this and other related adoption issues: www.adoption institute.org

Joanie Siegel, 52, adopted her daughter from the NYC foster care system. Her daughter jokes that some people have midlife crises and get Ferraris – Joanie got a teenager. In the span of two years, Joanie went from single to grandmother. The three of them live in Harlem. She is a Director of Health Services for a multi-service agency that provides, among other things, foster care services.

John M. Simmons, 49, is a Huffington Post contributor and the award-winning author of *The Marvelous Journey Home* and *To Sing Frogs.* Both books are based on experiences that he and his wife had while adopting children from Russia. In May of 2013, Simmons resigned from position as CEO/President of White Knight Fluid Handling, Inc, a high-tech semiconductor equipment company that he co-founded. He now spends his time writing, speaking and educating for orphan advocacy. He and his wife have three biological children, one who is adopted from the U.S. and five who are adopted from Russia. They live in Utah.

Maggie Lamond Simone, 52, is a national award-winning columnist and author. Her books include *From Beer to Maternity,* a USA Book News Finalist for humor, *and POSTED! Parenting, Pets and Menopause, One Status Update At A Time.* Her essays are included in *P.S. What I Didn't Say* (2009), multiple *Chicken Soup for the Soul* editions, *Cosmopolitan* magazine, and *Notebook: Magazine* (Australia). She is a professor of journalism and public speaking at SUNY Oswego, Oswego, N.Y., a monthly columnist for *Family Times* in Syracuse, N.Y., and a blogger for *The Huffington Post.* She has a 15-year-old son and a 13-year-old daughter.

Rachel Snyder has for decades relied on the written and spoken word to inspire individuals to deepen their hunger to evolve spiritually and to embrace full-spectrum lives. A devotee of the meandering path, she has, at turns, been a journalist, a direct marketing copywriter, a stall mucker, an innsitter, a community activist, a housecleaner, and a public elected official. She is the author of *365 Words of Well-Being for Women* (Contemporary Books/McGraw-Hill, 1997) and its Barnes & Noble reprint, *Words of Wisdom for Women* (2003). Her 2010 title, *Be Filled with Faith: Words of Well-Being to Strengthen Your Spirit,* was published by Blue Mountain Arts, who has also included her writing in greeting cards and more than a dozen anthologies. A poet outlier living in remote, rural southeastern Colorado, Snyder's unique brand of "intelligent inspiration" can be found on her blog, "be whole now," at www.rachelsnyder.wordpress.com.

Ellie Stoneley, 51, became a mother for the first time following IVF treatment at 47 ¾. Her world is now ruled and brightened by her miraculous daughter, Hope. Ellie is based in the UK where she often writes and talks in the media as a passionate advocate for breastfeeding, baby-led weaning and trusting your instincts when it comes to motherhood. Her award-nominated blog, *Mush Brained Ramblings* http://www.crazypregnantperson.com, followed her pregnancy and the traumas leading up to Hope's birth, and continues with her journey into motherhood. Ellie loves travelling with her daughter, sunshine, Bruce Springsteen and margaritas but most of all, hanging out tiny vests and dresses on the washing line.

Lori Pelikan Strobel, forever 49, lives with her husband of 27 years. She is also a mother to two adult daughters and a dog named Louie. She is a member of The Society of Children's Book Writers and Illustrators. Lori has worked as a pharmaceutical sales representative, Pilates instructor, community college teacher, and real estate agent. Her favorite job has been, and will always be, mom. You can currently find Lori walking her dog, Louie, blogging at *Book Body Soul*, or working hard on her upcoming book. She can be found at her blog, www. bookbodysoul.com.

Shana Sureck, 52, is an award-winning photographer and multimedia storyteller with studios in Florence, MA and Hartford, CT. Before starting her own business in 2009, she was a photographer at the Hartford Courant for 21 years. She is married to her besherte (Yiddish for "beloved"), with a daughter, 12, and two stepsons, 17 and 20, and lives in Northampton, MA. She can be reached at shana@shanasureck.com. Shana is the East Coast photographer for the art gallery show **NURTURE: Stories of New Midlife Mothers,** the first and only art show dedicated to presenting women choosing motherhood over 40, now traveling North America.

Laura Sussely-Pope, 53, is a lawyer, administrator for online community groups and social media consultant. She is the mother of Adam, 28 and Jacob, 12, born with Down syndrome. Laura is one of the featured mothers in the art gallery show *NURTURE: Stories of New Midlife Mothers.*

Karen Synesiou, 50, is the CEO of the Center for Surrogacy and Parenting, Inc., notably, the leading surrogacy center in the world. Karen is also a Mother of three children, conceived through IVF – a daughter (11) who is three years older than her twin brothers (8), who were all created from the same IVF cycle!

Tina Traster is an award-winning journalist whose work has appeared in newspapers, magazines, and literary journals such as *Audubon, Family Circle, HuffingtonPost.com,* the *New York Post,* and the *New York Times,* among many others. She is the author of the "Burb Appeal" column in the New York Post. Her essay "Love Learned," about bonding with her adopted Russian daughter, is anthologized in the collections *Living Lessons* and *Mammas and Pappas.* She lives in Valley Cottage, New York. Traster is 51 years old. Julia is 11.

Lora Freeman Williams is 45 years old and a freelance writer and coach to writers and entrepreneurs. She lives in Boulder, Colorado with her husband and 7-year-old son, Isaac. She has written and will soon publish *The Wilderness of Motherhood: A Memoir of Hope and Healing,* a book that expands upon the wilderness and parenting theme in this essay. Her website, www. wildernessofmotherhood.com, offers up-to-date reflections on parenting and the unfolding journey of recovery from PTSD.

Austin Wimberly, 40, is the adoptive father of four children from Russia. Inspired by his adoption experiences, his first novel, *Sobornost,* was published in 2012 and was a quarterfinalist for the 2013 Amazon Breakthrough Novel Award. He lives in Alabama with his wife, four children, a chocolate lab and black cat. When he isn't earning a living as a software engineer, parenting, or keeping peace between the dog and cat, he writes. He can be found at http://www.austinwimberly.com.

Jo Beth Young is a modern Medicine Woman whose channel for healing comes through her creativity. A natural intuitive she has passionately worked her unique take on practical spirituality, mystical experience and awakening to love for clients internationally. As a writer, musician and artist, Jo Beth co-created the Illumination Oracle of divine guidance that is rooted in ancient wisdom, folklore and the archetypal journey of the soul with writer and teacher Sally Teixeira. To learn more about her one-to-ones, speaking and events visit www.joannabeth.com or http://www.untothelighthouse.blogspot.co.uk/ for her writing on the journey of awakening.

26173799R00127

Made in the USA
Charleston, SC
26 January 2014